Pre-Workshop Tax Exam

Please complete before session begins.

1. Joan entertains some potential real estate managers for her rental properties. She spends $40 dollars on food and drinks. Which is the correct answer?

    a. Joan may deduct the $40 and does not need a receipt.
    b. Joan may deduct the $40, but needs a receipt as proof if audited.
    c. Joan may only deduct $30, but needs to keep a receipt if audited.
    d. Joan may only deduct $20 and does not need a receipt.
    e. Joan may only deduct $30, but does need a receipt for proof if audited.

2. Marc wants to deduct the cost of the play, "Socket to the IRS." For him to do this, tax law requires him to discuss business within what time frame of the play?

    a. Within 24 hours of the play.
    b. Within 48 hours of the play.
    c. Within 72 hours of the play.
    d. Within 90 hours of the play.
    e. Within the same week as the play.
    f. None of the above.

3. Tim wants to give a house warming gift costing $100 to one of his clients. Tim may deduct what portion of the business gift, assuming that he has appropriate documentation for the IRS?

    a. $100
    b. $50
    c. $40
    d. $25
    e. Nothing since business gifts aren't deductible.

4. Karen has several employees working in her business. If Karen has a birthday celebration for one of the employees and spends $200 on the party. How much of the $200 can she deduct? Assume that <u>no</u> company business was discussed.

    a. $200
    b. $100
    c. $80
    d. $25
    e. Nothing since it's a social party and not for business.

(continued on back)

1

5. John wants to take some business related courses on a cruise ship that cruises around the Hawaiian Islands. If he gets the appropriate documentation for the IRS by the cruise line, and spends a total of $3,000, how much of the cruise cost may he deduct?

    a. $3,000
    b. $2,000
    c. $1,000
    d. $500
    e. None of the above.

6. Mary has a business meeting in Vancouver B.C. Mary likes Vancouver so much that she spends another 5 days having fun for a total of 6 days away from home. Thus, she leaves home on Sunday from Oregon and comes home on Saturday. If her airfare was $600, how much of the airfare may she deduct?

    a. $600
    b. $250
    c. $100 (which is 1/6 of the airfare)
    d. Nothing since she didn't spend more that one-half of days on business.

7. Allie is attending a convention in Rome, Italy. She spends 7 days in Rome attending a 5 day convention. She also spends one day of travel to get there and one day getting back. If she dry cleans her clothing when she gets home and <u>not</u> at the convention, and spends a total of $150, how much of the $150 may she deduct?

    a. $150
    b. $75
    c. $37.50
    d. Zero
    e. None of the above.

8. In the US, you can deduct all qualified medical expenses not covered by insurance if they exceed a high threshold amount of 7.5% of your adjusted gross income. Wouldn't it be great if you could deduct all or most of your medical expenses as a business expense, which would be deductible at your top tax bracket? Well, you can with a Self-Insured Medical Reimbursement Plan. However, what is the limit imposed on these plans?

    a. $2,500 per person, per year, subject to reasonable wage test.
    b. $3,000 per person, per year, subject to reasonable wage test.
    c. $3,600 per person, per year, subject to reasonable wage test.
    d. $5,000 per person, per year, subject to reasonable wage test.
    e. No limitation, but subject to reasonable wage test.

9. Kevin puts seed and fertilizer on his home lawn each year. How should this be treated?

    a. Added to the basis of the home.
    b. Completely ignored since it does not constitute an improvement of the home.
    c. Deduct the cost of seed and fertilizer.
    d. Amortize the cost of seed and fertilizer over three years.
    e. Elect choice A or D.
    f. None of the above.

Tax Strategies for Business Professionals

By Sanford C. Botkin, C.P.A., *Esq.*

TAX REDUCTION INSTITUTE

TRI Seminars, Inc.
13200 Executive Park Terrace • Germantown, Maryland 20874
1-800-TRI-0-TAX • 1-800-874-0829
Visit our website at www.taxreductioninstitute.com
www.facebook.com/loweryourtaxes
www.twitter.com/sandytaxman

Please note all forms referenced in this publication are available at www.irs.gov by clicking on "Forms & Publications".

Special Thanks:
We wish to thank E. Geoffrey Sella, C.P.A. and Kevin Doyle, C.P.A. of Rockville, Maryland for their invaluable contribution. We also wish to thank Mike Sampson, Professor of Taxation at American University, for his valuable feedback.

Legal Notice: This workbook is for use with the workshop only. Neither the publisher nor the speakers are rendering tax, legal, accounting, or other professional advice. Tax strategies and techniques depend on an individual's facts and circumstances; accordingly, the information presented in this workshop must be correlated with the individual's tax situation to establish applicability. Moreover, because of the complexity of the tax laws, the constant changes resulting from new developments, and the necessity of determining appropriateness to a particular taxpayer, it is important that professional advice be sought before implementing the tax ideas suggested in this workshop.

Table of Contents

Glossary of Icons

Bright Idea

Great money saving idea that should be given serious consideration.

Hot Tip

A good idea that may give new insight.

Reminder

Important reminder to remember the point being made.

Warning

This is a problem of which you should be aware.

TRI Seminars, Inc.

TRI Seminars, Inc., dba the Tax Reduction Institute, is a tax education company located in Germantown, Maryland, a suburb of Washington, D.C., just a short distance from the IRS. TRI is involved in the creation and distribution of valuable tax information to business and professional people.

First and foremost, we are communicators and educators. We may take the subject of taxes seriously, but we don't take ourselves too seriously. Our presentations feature cartoons that maintain interest, humor that lightens the subject matter, and easy to follow examples which make it possible for you to gain immediate control of your taxes—and that means more money in your pocket!

Our speakers have been featured in major publications including *The Wall Street Journal, Money Magazine* and *Kiplinger Personal Finance Magazine* (formerly *Changing Times*). We have also appeared on shows including *Fox News, CBS News Nightwatch, Good Morning America, CNN* and the *Financial News Network*.

The Tax Strategies Seminar is an outstanding program designed to educate those who attend in numerous strategies to reduce tax liabilities. These proven techniques are invaluable tools to legally, morally and ethically reduce taxes.

In addition to the seminar, TRI launched a new Tax Reduction Diary to make it easy to comply with today's tough new documentation rules. IRS requires you to have a diary where you record the:

- Amount of each business expense

- Time it took place

- Location of the business activity

- Business purpose

- Business relationship of the person involved

The Tax Reduction Diary is a complete record-keeping system to help you do all of the above. It is also designed to save you money all year long. Why? Because it reminds you to record all those expenses that you often forget — tips, tolls, telephone, parking, etc.

TRI distributes the *TRI Talk Tax & Financial Update* newsletter. This newsletter updates the seminar material with the latest changes and incorporates ideas that have not been covered by the seminar. The ideas covered include business deduction strategies, real estate tax strategies, estate and probate planning, and fringe benefit planning.

Sanford C. Botkin

Sanford C. Botkin, Attorney, Certified Public Accountant, is Chief Executive Officer and principal lecturer of the Tax Reduction Institute.

During the past ten years, Mr. Botkin has taught more than 100,000 taxpayers how to save millions on their taxes with this seminar. He consistently earns rave reviews for his clear and humorous presentations.

Prior to joining the Tax Reduction Institute, Mr. Botkin spent three years in the tax department of the international accounting firm, Touche Ross. He has extensive financial and legal experience, including five years as a legal specialist in the Office of Chief Counsel for the Internal Revenue Service.

Mr. Botkin has also authored numerous technical articles for national publications, lectured to various professional and trade groups, and served as an Adjunct Professor of accounting and law at the University of Maryland and Columbia Union College. Mr. Botkin's outstanding teaching ability has consistently earned him excellent ratings. In fact, Mr. Botkin was one of eight attorneys selected by the Internal Revenue Service to train all new attorneys to the Internal Revenue Service's Corporate Tax Division.

Mr. Botkin is a member of the Florida Bar Association and the Florida Institute of Certified Public Accountants. He is also listed in *Who's Who in Business*.

Mr. Botkin can be heard on the syndicated radio show *Business Talk Soup* with John DeBevoise and has been featured on *Fox Business News*. He is also on the Wealth Mastery faculty of Robbins Research International (an Anthony Robbins company).

Finally, Sandy is the author of the best-selling books, *Lower Your Taxes Big Time,* and *Real Estate Tax Strategies of the Rich,* which are available at Amazon.com. Look for Sandy's latest release *Achieve Financial Freedom Big Time.*

"The art of taxation consists in so plucking the goose as to obtain the largest possible amount of feathers with the smallest amount of hissing."

— Jean Baptiste Colbert
French Finance Minister
Under Louis XIV, 1619–1683

"Whenever Congress is about to pass a tax reform bill, grab your wallet and run."

— Senator Symms of Idaho

1 Bullet Proof your Tax Records

Purpose of Seminar

Help your accountant: Our goal is not to make you into a tax accountant. Our goal is not to teach you how to fill out a tax form. Our goal is to help you identify your legitimate business deductions so you will be able to put your accountant in a position to help you.

Your responsibility: All of the numbers included in your tax return are your responsibility. You create the numbers, not your accountant. You are required to have adequate support for your tax return. When you sign your tax return, you attest to its accuracy under penalties of perjury. Moreover, you are required to read your return. You cannot avoid penalties by claiming that you solely relied on your accountant. When we state the words "Audit proof" or "Bullet Proof", our meaning is to significantly bulletproof your records from any audit adjustment. In other words, by following our advice to the letter, you should be able to substantially increase your outcome of any audit.[1]

Myth: There is a popular myth that "your accountant takes care of your taxes." We equate that to your doctor taking care of your body, your dentist taking care of your mouth, or your mechanic taking care of your automobile.

Your accountant: Your accountant depends on you for the numbers and information. Furthermore, your accountant charges by the hour, has many clients, and is very busy. You take your information to your accountant during the busiest time of the year. Consequently, your accountant does not have time for the "dawn to dusk" business deductions that are discussed during this workshop.

2015 Tax Rates[25]

Single Individuals
Standard Deduction = $6,300

Taxable Income Over	But Not Over	Pay +	% of Excess	Of the Amount Over
0	$9,225	0	10%	0
$9,225	$37,450	$922.50	15%	$9,225
$37,450	$90,750	$5,156.25	25%	$37,450
$90,750	$189,300	$18,481.25	28%	$90,750
$189,300	$411,500	$46,075.25	33%	$189,300
$411,500	$413,200	$119,401.25	35%	$411,500
$413,200	-	$119,996.25	39.6%	$413,200

Married Individuals Filing Joint Returns and Surviving Spouses
Standard Deduction = $12,600

Taxable Income Over	But Not Over	Pay +	% of Excess	Of the Amount Over
0	$18,450	0	10%	0
$18,450	$74,900	$1,845.00	15%	$18,450
$74,900	$151,200	$10,312.50	25%	$74,900
$151,200	$230,450	$29,387.50	28%	$151,200
$230,450	$411,500	$51,577.50	33%	$230,450
$411,500	$464,850	$111,324.00	35%	$411,500
$464,850	-	$129,996.50	39.6%	$464,850

Heads of Household
Standard Deduction = $9,250

Taxable Income Over	But Not Over	Pay +	% of Excess	Of the Amount Over
0	$13,150	0	10%	0
$13,150	$50,200	$1,315.00	15%	$13,150
$50,200	$129,600	$6,872.50	25%	$50,200
$129,600	$209,850	$26,722.50	28%	$129,600
$209,850	$411,500	$49,192.50	33%	$209,850
$411,500	$439,000	$115,737.00	35%	$411,500
$439,000	-	$125,362.00	39.6%	$439,000

Married Individuals Filing Separate
Standard Deduction = $6,300

Taxable Income Over	But Not Over	Pay +	% of Excess	Of the Amount Over
0	$9,225	0	10%	0
$9,225	$37,450	$922.50	15%	$9,225
$37,450	$75,600	$5,156.25	25%	$37,450
$75,600	$115,225	$14,693.75	28%	$75,600
$115,225	$205,750	$25,788.75	33%	$115,225
$205,750	$232,425	$55,662.00	35%	$205,750
$232,425	-	$64,989.25	39.6%	$232,425

1. The Personal Exemption for 2015 is $4,000;
   Personal Exemptions start to Phase Out for Single with AGI of $258,250 and Married with AGI of $309,900.

2. Itemized Deductions start to Phase Out for Singles with AGI of $258,250 and Married with AGI of $309,900.

3. $1,000 tax credit for each dependent child under age 17 in 2015:
   The credit is phased out by $50 for every $1,000 above the following thresholds;
   a) $75,000 for single taxpayers   b) $110,000 for married joint filing

4. 2015, Long Term Capital Gains & Dividends are taxed at the maximum rate of:
   • 0% for taxpayers in the 10% and 15% tax brackets
   • 15% for taxpayers in the 25%, 28%, 33% & 35% tax brackets
   • 20% for taxpayers in 39.6% tax bracket
   Plus 3.8% Medicare Surcharge on Net Investment Income for Threshold Income of over $200,000 for singles and over $250,000 for married

2015 Social Security Taxes for Self Employed and Employees

Self-Employed.. Tax of 15.3% on earnings through $118,500 for 2015.
Medicare Tax* of 2.9% on earnings over $118,500 with no limit
*Additional .9% on earnings over $200,000 single and $250,000 married

Employers & Employees... Employers pay 7.65% / Employees pay* 7.65% for 2015
*Employees pay additional .9% on earnings over $200,000 singles and $250,000 married

Total taxes paid by Bolen, a single sole proprietor who earned $80,000 taxable income

Dollars		Rate	
Federal Income Tax	$13,219	25%	
Social Security Tax	12,240	15.3%	(Net-after value of deductions)
State (DC) Income Tax	8,000	10%	(Net of the deduction)
Totals	$33,459	50.3%	

Visit our web site at: www.taxreductioninstitute.com

Our goal: During this seminar, we will help you create tax information and soundly constructed supporting records. We will raise some questions that you'll want to discuss with your accountant. Finally, we will help your accountant become more aggressive with your tax deductions.

We understand: We understand the condition of your paperwork. It's an extremely painful process keeping tax records in good order.

This workshop: This workshop will help you put some order into your tax records.

New tax habits: We will help you create new tax habits that will put more money into your pockets at the end of the tax year after you pay Uncle Sam.

Injection: We will also inject you with many new tax planning ideas and several new record-keeping ideas. The record-keeping suggestions may be a little painful but they will be good for you.

Inject your accountant: You will leave this seminar with tax planning ideas that will help your accountant.

Business Expenses

Business: Generally, you are allowed to deduct all ordinary and necessary business expenses.[2] The deduction depends on your ability to prove a profit motive.[3] Thus, you are not in business unless you are trying to produce a profit. When you are trying to make a profit, you may deduct your ordinary and necessary business expenses.

Ordinary and necessary: An ordinary and necessary expense is:

- Helpful[4] or appropriate[5] and
- Customary,[6] usual,[7] or normal[8]

The courts have deemed all ordinary expenses as necessary. However, an expense could be necessary but not ordinary and therefore not deductible.[9] Be advised, there is a case that notes that all expenses must be reasonable in amount and not lavish.

No personal, family, or living expenses: You may not deduct personal, family, or living expenses.[10] Allocations may be necessary to establish the dollar amount of business expenses.[11] In other cases, if there is any personal taint whatsoever, no business deduction is allowed.[12]

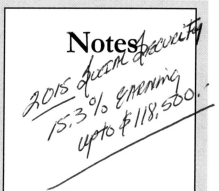

Notes

2015 Social Security
15.3% earning
upto $118,500.

     Visit our web site at: www.taxreductioninstitute.com

Notes

Why Documentation Is Needed

Key: Documentation is the key to sustaining your tax position.

Cemetery: Without documentation, you end up in the tax deduction cemetery, losing all of your bona fide deductions.

The law: Documentation is required by law.[13]

IRS statement: IRS states in its official publications that you must maintain records that support accurate tax returns. The records should be made at or near the time of the expense when there is accurate recall. Such records must be permanent, accurate, and complete.

Disallowance: Failure to meet the adequate documentation standards of the Internal Revenue Code can result in disallowance of your valid deductions.[14]

Guilty: IRS thinks you might cheat on your taxes; accordingly, you are assumed guilty until you prove you are innocent.

Burden of support is on you: IRS examiners are not required to help you keep records. You have total responsibility for proving your deductions.[15]

Own demise: Failure to meet the requirements costs you bona fide deductions.

Fraud: You now answer questions concerning your automobile mileage records under penalty of perjury.[16] Congress has instructed IRS to ask for fraud penalties when taxpayers don't have good records of automobile use.[17]

Big, big penalties: Failure to keep good records results in penalties, among others, equal to:

- 1/2% to 1% a month delinquency penalty during the period that you failed to pay the proper amount of tax[18]

- 20% of underpayment attributable to negligence or disregard of the rules or did not have a reasonable basis for the deduction[19]

- 75% of any underpayment attributable to fraud[20]

- You may not deduct some interests paid to the IRS if they were due to a business deduction on your Schedule C.[21]

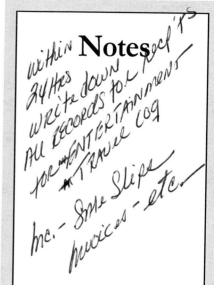

Notes

within 24 hrs write down rcpt's
All records for
for ★ ENTERTAINMENT
★ Travel Log
Inc. - Some Slips
invoices - etc.

The Proper Documentation System

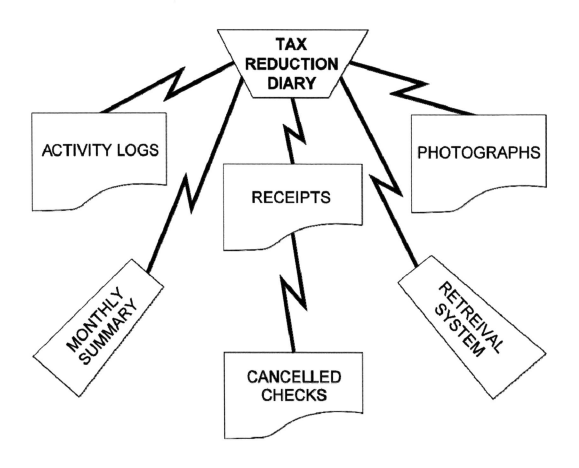

Strategies To Meet The Records Requirements

Strategy 1: Build a documentation system.

Three distinct records: Regardless of how you conduct your business, whether as a corporation or as a sole-proprietorship, you need three separate and distinct tax records:

- Permanent files
- Regular files
- A daily diary

Permanent files: Include your prior years' tax returns, stock purchases and sales, equipment purchases and sales, and similar entries. Generally, you want to keep any record that relates to more than one tax year in your permanent file. If you purchase property, your permanent files should include the purchase documents, closing statements, deeds, and other expenses related to the purchase.

Regular files: Include time sheets for part-time help, receipts, invoices, canceled checks, and other corroborative evidence.

Daily diary: Your daily diary — which can be your appointment book — is the focal point of your documentation system. This is especially true if you operate a personal service business. The smaller your business, the more important this document becomes. Your daily diary should include:

- All of your appointments
- Where and when you travel
- Where you go by automobile
- Where and when you entertain your business contacts

Strategy 2: Use three-part checks:

Keep a separate business checkbook and use three-part checks. Regardless of your business form, whether a corporation or sole-proprietorship, the three-part check is necessary to build good, easy-to-use records in your regular files.

1. Send part one, the original of the check, to the vendor.

2. Staple supporting evidence such as receipts or invoices to the yellow copy (part two) of the check and file alphabetically in the vendor file.

3. Put part three in a numerical file for later viewing by IRS and reference by you.

INVOICES — RATHER THAN RECP'TS

Record Retention Periods

General Rule: You must keep records in sufficient detail to establish the amount of income, deductions, and credits shown in any tax or information return.[1] You must keep them available for IRS inspection for as long as the contents may become material in the administration of any tax law.[2]

Flowchart For General Rule:

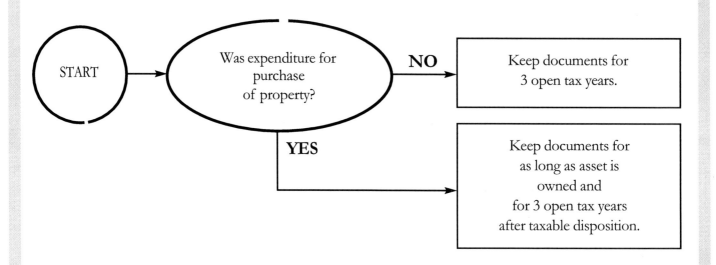

Three Year Rule: Generally, all income taxes must be assessed within three years from the date the return was filed or due, whichever is later.[3]

Extension By Agreement: The statute of limitations can be extended by a written agreement between you and IRS.[4]

Six Year Rule: If you omit an amount in excess of 25 percent of gross income shown in the return, a six year limitation period applies.[5]

No Limitation Rule: If you fail to file a return or file a fraudulent return, there is no statute of limitations.[6]

[1] Reg. § 31.6001-1(a)
[2] Reg. § 31.6001-1(e)
[3] IRC § 6501(a)
[4] IRC § 6501(c)(4)
[5] IRC § 6501(e)(1)(A)
[6] IRC § 6501(c)(1) & (3)

Strategy 3: Keep Form 1099 information separate. Negligence penalties are automatic if you fail to report all the income that's reported to IRS on Form 1099.[22] The negligence penalty applies to your total underpayment of tax, not just the portion due to negligence.[23] Any deposit that you make that would not normally be included in a 1099 or W-2 should be copied. Thus, if you get a large gift, insurance reimbursement, or transfer money from one account to another, make copies of the checks. Failure to do so may result in the IRS treating the deposit as income.

Strategy 4: Join the pack-rat brigade and pay less tax. 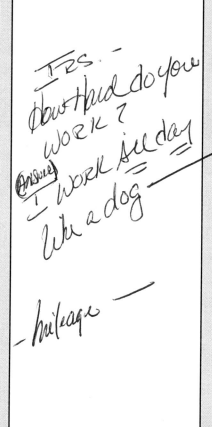 Save every receipt, whether personal or business, for all money spent. It's virtually impossible for you to know all of the receipts you are required to keep. Since you don't know what's important and what's not, it's safest to save everything for at least three years. Remember, you carry the burden of proof. It's rare that you can establish proof retroactively.[24]

Strategy 5: Use a business credit card. To keep your record-keeping burden to a minimum, use a separate charge card for all your business expenditures. The charge card copy acts as a receipt for your travel, entertainment, and gas and oil purchases. It also eliminates the need to make an audit trail for the deductible interest. By using one or more credit cards solely for business, you can deduct the finance charges on the business cards as well as the annual fees on all cards used solely for business.

Strategy 6: Think like a prosecuting attorney. You carry the burden of proof and your records are the evidence you gather. Think like a prosecuting attorney and put together all of your evidence in a fashion that unquestionably supports your deductions.

- An airline ticket shows the name of the passenger.

- An airline ticket shows the destination and any stops made en route to or from a business destination.

- Lodging receipts show single or double occupancy.

- Signatures on gasoline credit card charges can indicate use by family members other than the taxpayer.

- Repair bills can establish the accuracy of automobile mileage.

Hindsight: An audit of your tax return takes place almost 18 months after you have filed it. Your documentation system must be maintained on a daily basis, but in a manner that establishes intent for an entire year.

17

Notes

Notes

1. Bullet Proof Your Tax Records

1. <u>Walter Caughlin,</u> TC Memo 1994-113.

2. IRC § 162(a).

3. <u>Doggett v. Burnett,</u> 65 F.2d 191 (D.C. Cir 1933). See § 83 of the Internal Revenue Code.

4. <u>Commissioner v. Heininger,</u> 320 U.S. 467 (1943).

5. Ibid.

6. <u>Lilly v. Commissioner,</u> 343 U.S. 90 (1952).

7. Ibid.

8. Ibid. See also <u>Commissioner v. Heininger,</u> footnote 3 above: <u>Deputy v. Dupont,</u> 308 U.S. 488 (1939).

9. <u>Welch v. Helvering,</u> 290 U.S. 111 (1933).

10. IRC § 262.

11. Reg. § 1.162-2(b)(1); 1.162-5(d); 1.262-1.

12. <u>Thomas v. Commissioner,</u> 42 T.C.M. 328 (1981).

13. IRC § 6001.

14. <u>Rugel v. Commissioner,</u> 127 F.2d 393 (8th Cir. 1942).

15. Reg. § 31.6001-1(a).

16. See IRS Forms 2106, Employee Business Expenses, 4562, Depreciation and Amortization and declarations above the signature lines on Forms 1040, U.S. Individual Income Tax Return, and 1120 U.S. Corporation Income Tax Return.

17. Conference Committee Report on P.L. 99-44, as found in [1988] 8A Stand. Fed. Tax. Rpt. (CCH) ¶ 5528.034.

18. IRC § 6651(d)(1).

19. IRC § 6662+1.6662-7T(c) of the regulations.

20. IRC § 6653(b)(1)(A).

21. IRC § 6621(a)(2) but see <u>Redlark,</u> 106 T.C. Page 62 (over-turning the regulations), Aff'd U.S.T.C. par. 50, 322 (9th cir. 1998).

22. IRC § 6653 (a).

23. Reg. § 301.6653-1(c)(1)(i).

24. Rev. Proc 92-71 (1992-35 I.R.B. 17) (where checks in some circumstances are no longer needed to be kept where other appropriate evidence is available).

25. Rev. Proc 2003-86.

Notes

2 Maximize Your Deductible Entertainment Expenses

EVEN UNDER $75.- MAYBE Keep Recp't

Limits: Starting in 1994, tax law limits most of your entertainment expenses to 50%.[1]

Stiffer rules on the way: The new law also requires IRS to stiffen the documentation requirements for deductible entertainment expenses.[2]

Receipt rule: No receipts are required for <u>entertainment</u> expenses under $75 <u>per expense</u>.[3]

Strategy 1: Discuss business while you eat.   *BUSINESS IS Unbelievable[4] — NEVER HAVE ENOUGH*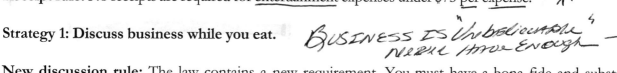

New discussion rule: The law contains a new requirement. You must have a bona fide and substantial business discussion just before, during, or after the business meal to qualify for a business meal deduction. The discussion clearly doesn't have to have a specific time limit or exceed the entertainment, but it must be substantial. What this seems to mean is that there must be a clear and specific business purpose. The key is that the primary motivation must be for business and not for personal reasons.[4] The same rule applies to all entertainment. Check with your accountant about this.

Specific advance purpose for the entertainment is required: You must have a specific business purpose to meet with your prospects in order to deduct any entertainment with them. The following examples illustrate this:

> **Example:** Sam goes to Outback Steakhouse alone for dinner. He strikes up a conversation with the waitress about his business. His dinner would not be deductible since he didn't have a prearranged appointment to meet her.

> **Example:** Same facts as above except that the waitress is Sam's next door neighbor. Sam discusses selling the waitress's house, but she doesn't have time to talk. Instead she suggests that Sam come to the restaurant where she works and talk about listing her home over lunch. This meal would be deductible.

Documentation of a Business Meal Followed By a Theatre Performance

Note how the theatre is **linked** to the meal with the word **followed**

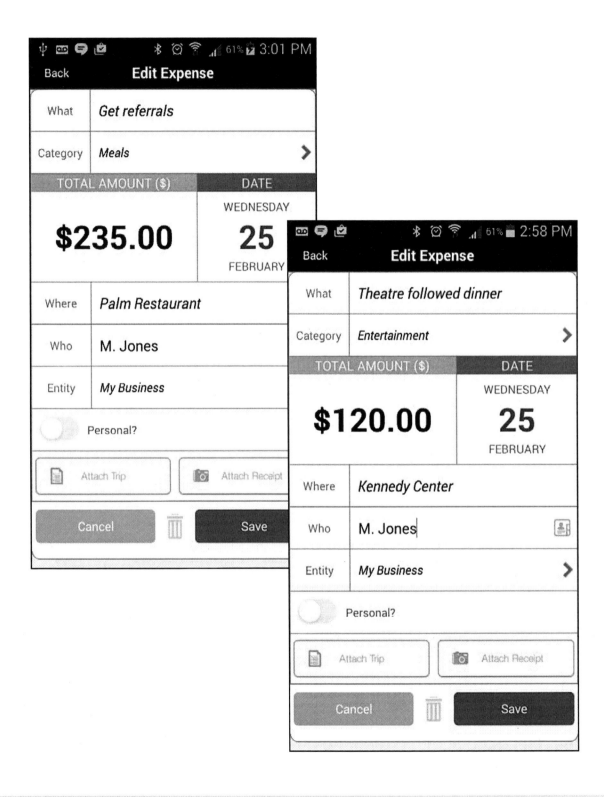

Setting: The business meal must take place in surroundings conducive to a business discussion.[6] IRS presumes that the active business discussion test is not met if the business meal occurs under circumstances where there is little or no possibility of engaging in business.[7] Eating dinner at a nightclub with a continuous floorshow is an example of a non-business setting.[8] Similarly, a large cocktail party is not a business setting.[9]

Documentation: Answering the questions "who," "where," and "why" and recording the cost as shown on the page on the left will give you proper documentation for business meals.

Strategy 2: Deduct theater tickets and other "associated entertainment" expenses.

Not a business setting: The theater is not a place conducive to a business discussion.[10] According to tax law, you may not claim a deduction for discussing business at the theater.[11]

Deduction rule: The cost of theater tickets is deducted under the "associated entertainment" rule.[12] Associated entertainment, also called goodwill entertainment, takes place in a nonbusiness setting.[13] No business discussion occurs during the entertainment. The entertainment precedes or follows a substantial and bona fide business discussion, usually the same day as the entertainment.[14]

Key-Record the link. There must be a link between the business discussion and the entertainment.[15] See the page on the left for an example of how the link is recorded. Note that the business discussion occurred in a proper business setting and was followed by entertainment associated with the dinner discussion. You also need to show the duration of the business discussion for any associated entertainment.

Note: Any entertainment of non-business guests who did not attend business meeting or training program would result in a disallowance of entertainment facilities costs. This limitation on deduction would apply to depreciation, rent, and operating expenses. Out of pocket expenses (meals or musicians) would be deductible.

Nonbusiness settings: Associated entertainment that can be linked to business meals and other direct business discussions includes entertainment at:

- Nightclubs
- Golf courses
- Theaters
- Sports events
- Hunting trips
- Fishing trips
- Ski trips

Notes

= fun
50% TALK BUSINESS
setting
24HR Period
following — or
precedes —

TAX TRACKER

Documentation of a Business Meal

Note how the **Who, Where,** and **Why** are detailed.

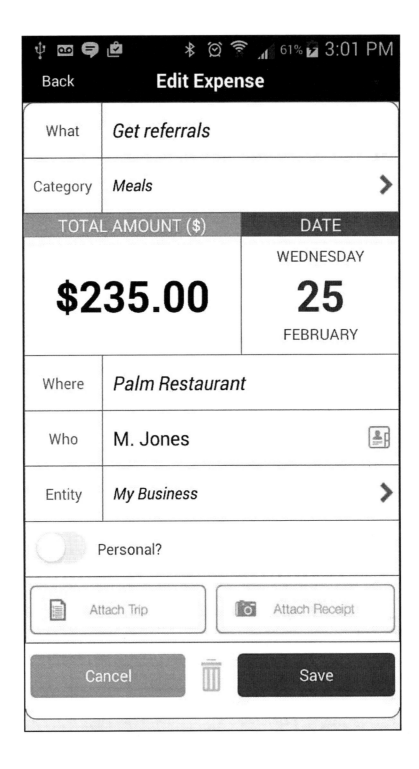

Note: 100% deduction for certain businesses: IRS uses an objective test to determine whether an activity is of a type to constitute entertainment (which is 50% deductible) or more like business pro- motion (which is 100% deductible). Thus, attending a movie or theatrical performance would normally be considered entertainment. However, it would be 100%deductible and not deemed entertainment, if done so by professional theater critics or movie critics.[16]

Similarly, a golf club salesman who plays golf and demonstrates his clubs and other golfing equipment should be able to deduct 100% of his green fees and costs of his golf balls, caddie expense, etc.

Strategy 3: Deduct season tickets by event. Season tickets and box seats to theaters and sports events are treated according to the individual events.[17] If, for example, you hold season theater tickets to attend 15 performances during the year, treat each of the 15 performances separately. The deduction is limited to the face value of the ticket. Scalper's profits are not deductible.

Strategy 4: Use entertainment tickets as business gifts to avoid $25 ceiling.

Property gift rule: Tax law limits your maximum deduction to $25 for business gifts to any one person during a tax year.[19] This limitation applies to gifts of tangible personal property.[20] Husband and wife are treated as one taxpayer for purposes of the $25 limit.[21] Gifts made, however, to businesses where there is no single person designated to receive or benefit from the gift, has no limit.[22]

Entertainment gift rule: Tax law has an alternate rule for gifts of entertainment tickets. You have the choice of treating the gift of a theater ticket either as entertainment or as a business gift.[23] There's no $25 limit on the entertainment gift. Moreover, when giving tickets as gifts, you need not go along to the entertainment event.[24]

Example: Mark gives theater tickets as a gift to a client. The total cost of the tickets is $175. Since the gift can be considered entertainment, it is subject to the 50% entertainment limit and not the $25 gift limit. Mark can deduct $87.50 (50% of $175).

Meals are not entertainment: Gifts of entertainment meals are no longer allowed.[25] You are entitled to a tax deduction for a business meal only if you are present during the consumption process.[26]

Strategy 5: Feed and entertain your spouse: IRS has a "closely connected" rule. Most spouses are closely connected. The closely connected rule permits deducting the expenses of entertaining your spouse as well as the spouse of a business guest.[27] In other words, if your business guest brings a spouse, you are entitled to bring yours.[28] Naturally, you must be entertaining the business guest during the ordinary and necessary course of your business and you must meet the business discussion and documentation requirements.

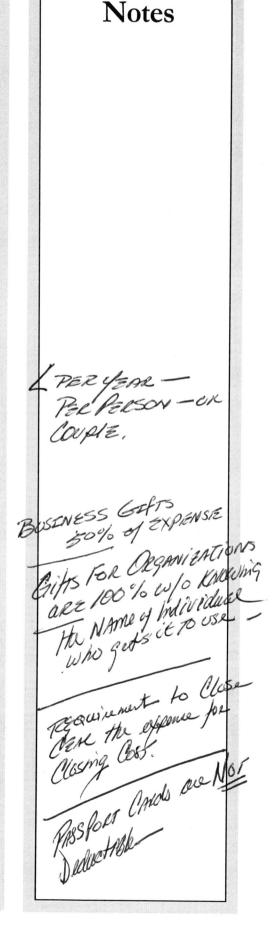

Notes

$ PER YEAR — PER PERSON — OR COUPLE.

BUSINESS GIFTS 50% of EXPENSE

Gifts FOR ORGANIZATIONS ARE 100% w/o knowing the NAME of Individual who gets it to use

requirement to close out the expense for Closing Cost.

Passport Cards are NOT Deductible.

VIP

The Five Substantiation Requirements For All Business Entertainment

⑥ *WHAT TYPE of EXPENSE*

General Rule: All business entertainment must meet the five elements of substantiation to qualify for a deduction. It makes no difference what other types of support you have for your business entertainment; failure to meet the five elements will result in disallowance.

1. **Cost:** The cost of each entertainment expenditure must be recorded someplace. When the cost is $75 or more, documentary evidence such as a receipt, voucher, or credit card charge copy must be retained to support expenditures.

2. **Time:** The definition of time is usually the date when the entertainment takes place. When entries are made in a diary-type document, the date on the diary page is adequate support for time.

3. **Description:** The nature and place of the entertainment ("business meal at Greasy Lloyd's") must be described. When a charge slip or receipt is obtained, the nature and place are usually self-evident.

4. **Business purpose:** Of the five elements, this is the most important. State the exact nature of the business discussion or activity. Be brief, but specific.

5. **Business relationship:** IRS wants you to identify the person or persons entertained. The names, occupations, official titles, and other corroborative information to establish the business relationship should be identified. In many cases, the person's name with the word "prospect" would be sufficient to establish both business purpose and business relationship for a business meal.
   Ⓧ *— WHO —*

Timely Recording: The recording must be contemporaneous with the activity. For all practical purposes, that means you must record the five elements of substantiation on a timely basis, preferably on the day the entertainment takes place.

The Five Substantiation Requirements For Business Meals

Entry in Diary:

What	Obtain referrals
Category	Meals >
TOTAL AMOUNT ($)	**DATE**
20.00	WEDNESDAY **25** FEBRUARY
Where	Palm
Who	S. Jones

Notation on bottom of Charge Card Receipt:

```
              PALM RESTAURANT

ACCOUNT #  :  3175125698XXX   10/XX
TYPE       :  All American Charge
AUTH #     :  06138

SALE          $      17.43
TIP           $       2.57
TOTAL         $      20.00

X  William Taxpayer
      I AGREE TO PAY THE ABOVE AMOUNT
   ACCORDING TO THE CARD ISSUE AGREEMENT
      Bill Jones, TRP
      Obtain Referrals
```

Strategy 6: Deduct dutch treat meals.

When you go to a meal with a business guest, pay your own way and spend more than what you would normally spend,[29] the Dutch treat rule comes into play. If, for example, you attend a Chamber of Commerce luncheon meeting and the lunch costs more than you would normally spend for lunch, you may claim the excess as a dutch treat business lunch.

Example: You spend $22 at a Chamber luncheon. Had you not gone to the luncheon, you would have spent $2. Your deduction is $10; 50% of the excess business cost over your personal cost.

Strategy 7: Document personal meal costs to support your dutch treat meals and avoid the "Sutter Rule."

Written evidence: Your personal meal evidence must be in writing. Entries in your diary or account book are strong evidence.[30]

30-Day test: Record the cost of personal lunches in your diary. Do this for at least 30 personal lunch days during the year.

Meals at home: When you eat meals at home, the task of developing your personal meal costs is somewhat more complicated. There are basically two ways to compute the cost of personal meals consumed at home.

Method 1: Write down the actual items consumed and determine the cost of each item. Two eggs for breakfast, when a dozen eggs cost $1.20, would cost $.20. If you need to determine actual costs only a few times during the year, it's easy to simply write down the actual items consumed.

Method 2: Use grocery bills to make an allocation by members of the family. If, for example, the grocery bill for a week amounts to $150, you can estimate the cost for breakfast, lunch, and dinner. If the dinner groceries cost $70, you could divide the $70 by seven days in a week to arrive at $10 for the average dinner. If there are two people in your family, the average cost per person is $5. That would be your cost for purposes of determining your Dutch treat deductions and maximum disallowance under the Sutter Rule.

Recording the Cost of Group Entertainment At Home

Facts: Ritter built his own office building and is looking for tenants. He throws a party for friends that would be desirable tenants.

Entry in Diary

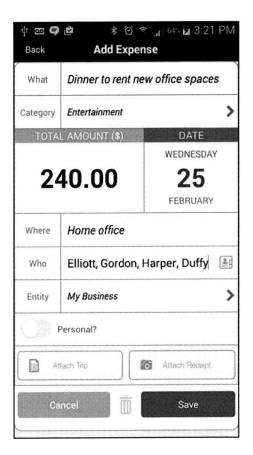

Results: Deductible Because Ritter Passes Tests 1 and 2

Test 1 — Clear showing of commercial motivation: Ritter's invitation established the introduction of the new office building as the reason for the party. In the room where the party was held, Ritter had photographs of the new building posted on a bulletin board. Although none of the individuals attending the party rented space in the new building, Ritter clearly established a business motivation for the party.

Test 2 — Meet five elements of substantiation:

1. **Cost:** Receipts and cancelled checks
2. **Time:** Date at top of diary page
3. **Description:** Words in diary
4. **Business purpose:** Words in diary plus invitations and photographs of people around the bulletin board
5. **Business relationships:** Names of individuals who own their own businesses and are prospective tenants

The Sutter Rule: IRS may at its whim invoke the Sutter Rule. The Sutter Rule allows IRS to disallow a portion of your business meals when such meals absorb substantial amounts of your typical living expenses.[31]

Strategy 8: Audit proof your entertainment deductions.

Entertainment must be incurred in the ordinary and necessary course of your business[32] and then documented to meet IRS substantiation requirements.[33] Failure to meet the requirements causes a loss of valid deductions.[34]

Strategy 9: Deduct home entertainment.

Your home is already a setting conducive to a business discussion.[35] If you invite a couple to your home for dinner, it's easy to have a one-on-one conversation. You do not need to spend more time trying to conduct business than you spend entertaining your guest.[36]

Example and elaboration: You invite Jones to your home to ask for a referral. You ask for and receive the referral. Even though 90% of the evening is spent on nonbusiness activities, the cost is deductible. If you asked for and failed to get a referral, the cost of entertainment is still deductible.

Strategy 10: Give small parties at home.

Your home entertainment deductions are secure when you discuss business with your guests.[37] You should not discuss business with closely connected spouses and significant friends.[38] Keep your guest list small (fewer than 12 people). Then you can talk to everyone with whom you need to discuss business.

Strategy 11: Properly set up and document large group entertainment to solidify deductions.

General Rule: When you invite more than 12 people to your home, you will be hard-pressed to prove to IRS that you had business discussions with everyone in attendance. Therefore, you must establish some other type of commercial motivation.

Notes

Personal celebrations are the plague: Never, never combine a personal event with a business entertainment event. A birthday party for your 10-year-old with business guests in attendance won't cut the mustard with IRS.[39] Home entertainment, especially when large groups are involved, is deductible only when you can firmly establish a business purpose.[40]

Display products: If you entertain a group for the purpose of showing a display of your business products or services, commercial motivation is generally clearly established.[41] When you combine the display of products with an invitation that invites the guests for a specific business reason, you improve your chances for deductibility.[42] Finally, if you have no personal or social relationships with the guests (other than business), your chances for a deduction are improved.[43]

Strategy 12: Give parties for employees. The reasonable cost of a year-end holiday party or a summer outing for employees and their families is 100% deductible.[44] There's no reduction to 50% of monies spent.[45]

Strategy 13: Provide lunches for employees. Under a recent law change, you may provide lunches to employees on a tax-free basis if you provide lunch for over one-half of the employees, and either;[46]

    1. there is a short lunch period[47] (generally no more than 45 minutes)

    2. they are available for emergencies[48] (such as an ambulance service)

    3. there are insufficient eating facilities nearby[49]

Also, meals must be furnished on normal business days.[50]

Strategy 14: Deduct business club dues and lunches.

You deduct dues paid to business clubs when such payment is in the ordinary and necessary course of business.[51] The term "ordinary and necessary" mean that the expenses are customary, usual or normal, and helpful or appropriate.[51] Dues to your local Chamber of Commerce would almost always be appropriate and normal.[53] Dues paid to professional societies are deductible.[54] Trade association dues are deductible if the association's purpose is the furthering of the business interests of its members.[55] Dues to community clubs organized to attract tourists and new members to your locality give rise to deductible dues.[56]

Notes

Note: Meals incurred and paid for while talking business at the club are deductible.

Strategy 15: Give sales seminars and presentations at home.

In a tax court decision,[57] the court ruled that all food and refreshments served to prospects were 100% deductible if provided at home during a sales seminar or sales presentation.

Entertainment Summary

Strategy 1:   Discuss business when you eat.

Strategy 2:   Deduct theater tickets and other associated entertainment expenses.

Strategy 3:   Deduct season tickets by event.

Strategy 4:   Use entertainment tickets as business gifts to avoid $25 ceiling.

Strategy 5:   Feed and entertain your spouse.

Strategy 6:   Deduct dutch treat meals.

Strategy 7:   Document personal meal costs to support your dutch treat meals and avoid the Sutter Rule.

Strategy 8:   Audit proof your entertainment deductions.

Strategy 9:   Deduct home entertainment.

Strategy 10:   Give small parties at home.

Strategy 11:   Properly set up and document large group entertainment to solidify deductions.

Strategy 12:   Give parties for employees.

Strategy 13:   Provide lunches for employees.

Strategy 14:   Deduct business club dues and lunches.

Strategy 15:   Give sales seminars and presentations at home.

Notes

2. Maximize Your Deductible Entertainment Expenses

1. IRC § 274(n).
2. H. Rept. 99-841, p. II-27.
3. Section 1.274-5(c) of the Regulations; IR 95-56; Notice 95-50, 1995-42 IRB.
4. Reg. § 1.274-2(d)(1), 1.274-2(d)(3)(i) of the ITR. See also Rev.Rul. 63-144, Q&A 35, 1963-2-CB 129 and <u>Harry Laforge vs. Comm</u>, 48 TC 358 (1967).
5. IRC § 274(a).
6. Reg. § 1.274-2(f)(2)(i)(a).
7. Reg. § 1.274-2(c)(7).
8. Reg. § 1.274-2(c)(7)(ii)(a).
9. Ibid.
10. Ibid.
11. Ibid.
12. Reg. § 1.274-2(d).
13. Reg. § 1.274-2(d)(1).
14. Reg. § 1.274-2(d)(1)(ii).
15. Reg. § 1.274-2(d)(3)(i)(a).
16. 1.274-2(b)(i)(ii).
17. Rev. Rul. 63-144, 1963-2 C.B. 129, Q & A 50.
18. Ibid.
19. IRC § 274(b)(1).
20. IRC § 274(j)(3)(A).
21. IRC § 274(b)(2)(B).
22. § 1.274-3(e)(2).
23. Reg. § 1.274-2(b)(1)(i); Reg. § 1.274-2(b)(1)(iii)(b).
24. Reg. § 1.274-2(b)(1)(iii)(b)(2).
25. IRC § 274(k)(2).
26. IRC § 274(k)(1)(B).
27. Reg. § 1.274-2(d)(4). Rev. Rul. 200-45, IRB 200-41: 46 RIA <u>Weekly Alert</u>, Number 39 (9/21/2000)
28. Ibid.
29. E.g., <u>Sutter v. Commissioner</u>, 21 T.C. 170 (1953), acq. 1954-1 C.B. 6.
30. Reg. § 1.274-5(c)(2).
31. Rev. Rul. 63-144, Q & A 31, 1963-2 C.B. 129; <u>Sutter v. Commissioner</u>, 21 T.C. 170 (1953), acq. 1954-1 C.B. 6.
32. IRC § 162(a).
33. IRC § 274(d).
34. Ibid.

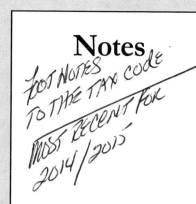

Notes

FOOT NOTES TO THE TAX CODE MOST RECENT FOR 2014/2015

35. Reg. § 1.274-2(e)(2).

36. Reg. § 1.274-2(f)(2)(i)(b).

37. Reg. § 1.274-2(d)(4); Rev. Rul. 63-144, 1963-2 C.B. 129, 136-37, Q & A 26-28.

38. Ibid.

39. Reg. § § 1.274-2(c)(4); 1.274-2(c)(7)(ii).

40. Reg. § 1.274-2(c)(4).

41. Ibid.

42. Ibid.

43. Steel v. Commissioner, 28 T.C.M. 1301 (1969).

44. H. Rept. 99-842, p. II-28.

45. Ibid.

46. IRC § 1.119(b)(4).

47. IRC § 1.119-1(a)(2)(ii)(b).

48. IRC § 1.119-1(a)(2)(ii)(a).

49. IRC § 1.119-1(a)(2)(ii).

50. IRC § 1.119-1(a)(2)(i).

51. IRC § 274(a)(2)(C).

52. Welch, Thomas v. Helvering, (1933, S Ct) 12 AFTR 1456, 290 US 111; Blackmer, Sidney v. Com., (1934, CA2) 13 ATFR 957, 70 F2d 255; Union Ganadera Regional De Chihuahua Inc, (2000) TC Memo 2000-357; Vaksman, Fabian, (2001) TC Memo 2001-165. Infact, Welch seems to imply thatan expense can be necessary and not ordinary to most similar businesses.

53. IRC § 274(a)(2)(C).

54. Reg. § 1.274-2(e)(3)(ii).

55. Reg. § § 1.274-2(e)(3)(ii); 1.274-2(f)(2)(i).

56. Roland J. Hymel, Jr., 86-1 U.S.T.C. ¶ 9419, CA-5 (1986).

57. Robert Matlock v. Commissioner, T.C. Memo 1992-324.

3 Combine Personal Pleasure With Business Travel

What Is Travel?

Definition: According to IRS, you are "traveling" when you are away from home overnight or for a period of time sufficient to require sleep.[1]

Example: You live in Washington, D.C., fly to New York City in the morning, and return that evening. You are not "traveling."[2] You were not away from home overnight.

Transportation trip: Your trip to New York City is classified by tax law as a non-travel trip. On this trip, you are allowed to deduct only your transportation costs.[3] You get no deductions for your meal expenses.[4]

Two categories: Travel expenses are divided into two distinct categories:

- Transportation expenses
- On the road expenses

Each category has its own separate rule base. It's possible to take a business trip where transportation expenses are not deductible but on the road expenses are deductible.

Transportation expenses: Transportation costs include the expenses you incur in getting to and from your destination.[5]

Notes

RELATED
RESOURCE

On the road expenses: Your on the road expenses include all costs necessary to sustain life while on your t_1. On the road expenses include lodging, meals, laundry, dry cleaning, and similar expenses.[7]

Expenses allowed: Tax law allows business travel deductions at 100% except for travel meal costs which are limited to 50% of your legitimate expenditures.[8] If you spend $50 for meals during travel, you're allowed to deduct only $25.

Receipt rule: No receipts required for travel expenses under $75 per expense with the exception of lodging.[9]

The primary purpose of the trip must be for business: For any travel to be deductible, you must have a specific business purpose BEFORE you go on the trip and the primary purpose of the trip must be for business. Thus, if your primary purpose is to attend your daughter's wedding or to attend Disney World, this trip would not be deductible even if you make some business contacts while you are there. On the other hand, if the primary purpose was to set up referrals, meet prospects, etc. and you had some incidental fun (such as going to Disney World), this trip would, in my opinion, be deductible. As you can see, this is a grey area.

Keep all receipts and be honest as to the expenses: I do note that IRS states in their regulations that no receipts are required for travel (other than lodging) or entertainment if under $75 per expense. As a practical matter, I keep all receipts anyway. However, if you lose some and they fall into these categories then don't worry. Also, I am NOT suggesting that you deduct any amount if under $75. If you spend $30 then you would deduct $30 subject to any limitation such as the 50% limit on food. Do NOT add more in expenses than you spend! Be accurate and honest. Don't violate the P.I.G. rule.

Overall Strategies To Increase Travel Deductions and Add More Pleasure

Strategy 1: Hire your spouse. If you want to take trips with your spouse, and deduct travel expenses for both of you, you must have a legitimate business reason for bringing along your spouse.[10] If your spouse is in an entirely different business than you, taking your spouse to one of your business conventions would not result in tax deductions for your spouse.

However, starting in 1994, if your spouse and/or dependents:
1) is a bona fide employee of your business,
2) is traveling for a bona fide business purpose, *and*
3) the expense would otherwise be deductible, you can obtain a tax deduction for traveling together.

If your spouse is licensed in your business and needs the information contained in the convention or seminar for continuing education for his/her license, they may attend the convention and deduct these expenses on his/her own tax return.

Strategy 2: Use business car for family travel.

Car expenses: Tax law allows you to deduct the cost of your business trip.[11] If you travel with nonbusiness family members, you are allowed to deduct the cost that you would have incurred had you taken the trip alone.[12] Since traveling with a full car costs no more than traveling alone, all of your business car expenses are deductible, even if you have nonbusiness passengers.

Lodging and meal expenses: When it comes to lodging and meals, you deduct all of your costs as if you had taken the trip alone.[13] If the motel cost is $60 for one occupant and $70 for the family, you deduct $60. The $10 differential is a personal, nondeductible expense.

...rt for Deducting Transportation Expenses When Trip ...es Business With Pleasure

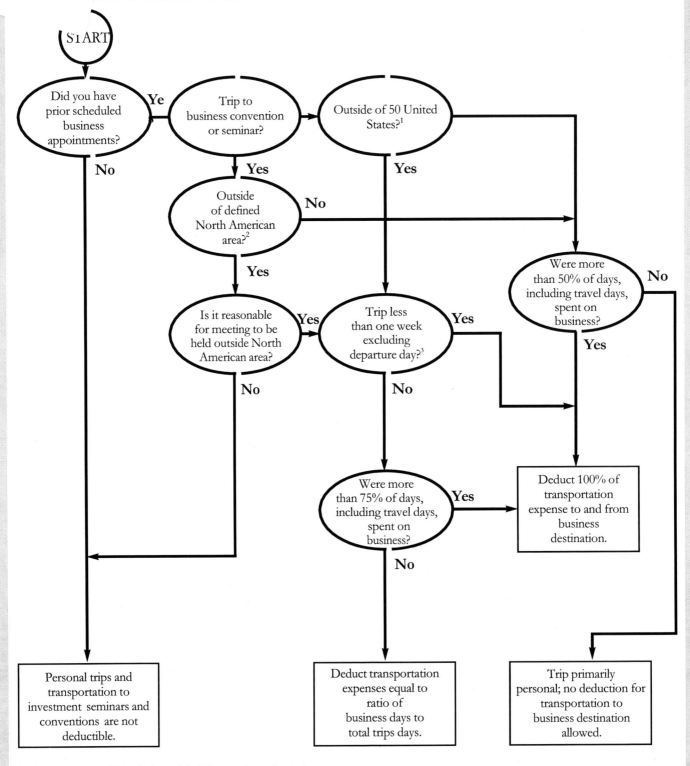

START

Did you have prior scheduled business appointments? **Yes** → Trip to business convention or seminar? → Outside of 50 United States?[1]

Did you have prior scheduled business appointments? **No** ↓

Trip to business convention or seminar? **Yes** ↓ Outside of defined North American area?[2]

Outside of 50 United States?[1] **Yes** ↓

Outside of defined North American area?[2] **No** →

Outside of defined North American area?[2] **Yes** ↓ Is it reasonable for meeting to be held outside North American area?

Is it reasonable for meeting to be held outside North American area? **Yes** → Trip less than one week excluding departure day?[3]

Is it reasonable for meeting to be held outside North American area? **No** ↓

Trip less than one week excluding departure day?[3] **Yes** →

Trip less than one week excluding departure day?[3] **No** ↓ Were more than 75% of days, including travel days, spent on business?

Were more than 50% of days, including travel days, spent on business? **No**

Were more than 50% of days, including travel days, spent on business? **Yes**

Were more than 75% of days, including travel days, spent on business? **Yes** → Deduct 100% of transportation expense to and from business destination.

Were more than 75% of days, including travel days, spent on business? **No** ↓

Personal trips and transportation to investment seminars and conventions are not deductible.

Deduct transportation expenses equal to ratio of business days to total trips days.

Trip primarily personal; no deduction for transportation to business destination allowed.

---

[1] Includes the District of Columbia but excludes U.S. possessions and territories.

[2] Trip outside Canada, Mexico, Jamaica, Barbados, Grenada, the U.S., its possessions, the Trust Territory of the Pacific, the Marshall Islands, the Federated States of Micronesia, Jarvis Island, Johnston Island, Kingman Reef, Costa Rica, Dominica, Dominican Republic, Guyana, Honduras, Saint Lucia, Trinidad, Tobago and Palau. See Section 274(b)(3) and Rev. Rul. 87-95, 1987-2 C.B. 79 and Rev. Rul. 94-56, 1994-36 IRB.

[3] Assuming one deductible business day during the trip; Reg. § 1.274-4(c).

Strategy 3: Drive 300 miles a day toward your business destination.

The Federal government reimburses IRS employees a full days per diem for each 300 miles of travel.[14] Take advantage of this rule. Plan your trips to cover 300 miles a day in direct route to your business destination. Each such day will count as a full business day and also allow you to deduct your on the road expenses for the day.

Strategy 4: Deduct dirty clothes.

Your deductible on the road expenses include the cost of getting clothes cleaned and laundered.[15] Question: Do you need to get the clothes cleaned or laundered while you are away from home in order to deduct the expense? No! What counts is where the clothes get dirty. If the clothes were soiled as a result of travel, you may get them cleaned at home and still deduct the cost.

Strategy 5: Take U.S. cruise ships.

If you are looking for a vacation cruise ship subsidy, this is it. You, and possibly your spouse, can deduct up to $2,000 each year for attending cruise ship conventions directly related to your business provided:[16]

- The cruise ship is registered as a U.S. vessel[17]

- All ports of call are in the United States or possessions of the United States[18]

- You submit two supporting statements with your tax returns[19]

- You pass the 51/49 test and keep good documentation.[20] See flowchart on page 40.

Strategies to Lock In And Increase The Amount Of Transportation Deductions

Overview: Transportation expenses are deductible when you take a deductible trip. The "trip" refers to the number of days you are away from home. Tax law then looks at the number of days away from home spent on business and applies a rule.

Flowchart of transportation expense rules: The flowchart on the left summarizes the transportation rule portion of the travel rules and tells you what percentage, if any, of the transportation costs are deductible.

Notes

155 Dry Cleaning Bill Immediately After Returning from Business Seminar

Notes

Strategy 6: Make weekends deductible.

Rule to follow: Tax law's strictest travel rules apply to trips to foreign destinations.[21] By following the strict rules in IRS Publication 463 chapter *Travel Outside the United States*, you eliminate confusion and lock in your U.S. travel deductions.

Set Friday and Monday meetings to surround the weekend: When you are traveling to a foreign destination, you may count as business days all weekends and legal holidays that fall between business meeting days.[22] That's important for two reasons;

- You deduct all on the road expenses for the weekends and holidays.[23]

- You add business days for purposes of determining if your transportation expenses are deductible.[24]

Example: Thelma leaves for a convention in Hawaii on Sunday and returns home on Friday night at a cost of $1,200 in airfare. If she chooses to stay over Saturday night and come home on Sunday, her airfare is reduced to $425 (thus saving $775). As long as her food and lodging for Friday, Saturday and Sunday are less than $775, she may count Friday, Saturday and Sunday as business days.

General rule for the United States: When traveling in the United States, you can count weekend days as business days when it would cost more to return home than to stay at your business destination.[25]

Example: You live in Buffalo and travel to Honolulu on Thursday, conduct business on Friday, must wait through the weekend for a business discussion on Monday, and then return to Buffalo on Tuesday. All days are counted as business days.[26] You deduct both your transportation expenses and your on the road expenses for all days, including the weekend.[27]

Observation: You obtain tax deductions for two days of fun and sun.

Stay Over Saturday and Sunday to reduce costs: In a private ruling[28] dated June 10, 1992, the IRS allowed Saturday and Sunday to be considered business days if the costs of staying over was less than the airfare savings of traveling past Saturday nights.

Notes

CHECK FOR SEMINARS BEING HELD IN THE AREA

Sandwich between Friday & Monday

Stay over Saturday Night to reduce cost. —

Notes

Strategy 7: Count travel days as deductible business days.

Travel days: Days in transit are considered business days provided that the travel is by reasonably direct route to the business destination and does not involve substantial non-business diversions.[29]

Two benefits: When a day is classified as a business day, you obtain the following tax benefits:

- Deductions for your on the road expenses
- A day counted toward satisfaction of the business trip test

Pick any means of transportation: The need to take a reasonably direct route does not affect your means of transportation. You may take the trip by automobile, airplane, boat, or train.[30] The days you spend traveling by direct route are considered business days.[31]

Special rule for luxury boats: The allowable deduction for luxury water travel may not exceed twice the highest amount generally allowable per day to a low-ranking White House employee traveling in the lower 48 United States, multiplied by the number of days you spend on the ship.[32]

Example: You take the Queen Elizabeth II from New York City to London. Your deduction may not exceed twice the White House per diem rate per day[33] for the continental US. If the White House per diem is $339,[34] your deduction for the six-day trip may not exceed $4,068 ($678 X 6 days).

Strategy 8: Add pleasure to other work days without loss of deductions.

Presence required: If your presence is required at a particular place for a specific and bona fide business purpose, that day is counted as a business day, even if your presence is required for only part of the day.[35] This applies even if you spend more time sightseeing during the normal working hours than participating in business activities.[36]

Convention and seminar days: If a convention or a seminar has at least six hours of scheduled business activities during the day, and you attend at least two-thirds of those activities, your day is considered a business day.[37] We call this the "Four-hour and one-minute rule."

Notes

NOTES
WORKBOOKS
3485 for Records.
-Agenda
-

Notes

Principal activity: If you spend the majority of the working hours pursuing your trade or business (generally, four hours and one minute), that day is counted as a business day.[38] When you are prevented from engaging in the conduct of your trade or business because of circumstances beyond your control, the day is still counted as a business day, even if you spend the day playing in the sand and enjoying the sun.[39]

Strategies That Identify More Reasons to Travel for Business with Pleasure

Strategy 9: Look after your real estate.

General rules: Real estate caretaking travel, if necessary, is deductible.[40] The "if necessary" part depends on your facts and circumstances. If you collect the rents and actively participate in the day-to-day operations of the rental property, you will obviously have to take some trips to make sure that the property is in good condition. You will also have to check on rents in the area, make repairs, and speak with certain vendors.

Management Company: Even if you engage a management company to look after the property, you must check on the management. Are they maintaining the property? Is the rent reasonable? How do the tenants feel about the management company? How does the management company feel about the tenants? It could take several days to get the answers to all these questions.

Repair days: Any day that you spend repairing and maintaining your property on a full-time basis is not counted as a day of personal use of the property.[41] Moreover, even if people related to you use the property for recreation on the same day, the day is not a personal day.[42]

Strategy 10: Visit colleagues.

Rationale: You can learn new business skills from your colleagues. Therefore, you can design your combined business and pleasure trips to make the rules work for you.

Notes

Example: You live in Washington, D.C., and take a trip to Dallas, Phoenix, San Francisco, Denver, Minneapolis, and Pittsburgh. At each location, you spend a few days visiting with colleagues to learn new business skills. You take the trip by automobile and drive at least 300 miles each day in direct route to the next business location.

Results: If you had no pleasure days or side trips, all days are business days. You deduct your on the road business expenses and your transportation costs.

Strategy 11: Get educated out of town. Tax law allows deductions for travel to and from educational facilities, meetings, seminars, and conventions.[43] If the same seminar is held both in your hometown and at a nice out-of-town resort, there is no requirement that you stay at home.

Strategy 12: Hunt for a job.

The rules: IRS allows deductions for all expenses directly related to a search for employment in the same trade or business. It makes no difference if the search is successful or unsuccessful.[44]

Documentation: You should have documentation of your intention to search for a job prior to your trip. Correspondence before the trip should be maintained in your files. Also, correspondence after the trip should be kept in the files.

Strategies for Audit Proofing Your Travel Deductions

Strategy 13: Keep the proper receipts.

Lodging receipts required: To prove that you have been away from home overnight or long enough to require sleep, you are required to keep all lodging receipts for travel.[45] In addition to showing that you are away on a trip that required sleep, the lodging receipt will let IRS know whether you are alone or with someone else.[46] Lodging receipts usually show the number of occupants in the room, a fact pointed out to IRS auditors.

Receipts for all expenses of $75 or more: Besides lodging receipts, you must have receipts for any other expenditures of $75 or more.[47] If you do not keep a good daily diary, you need receipts for expenditures that are less than $75. You may not simply make approximations when you are traveling.[48]

IRS Standard Allowance: If you do not want to keep receipts for meals and incidental costs (such as tips) incurred while traveling, courts have allowed self-employed taxpayers to use the IRS standard rates for meals and incidentals, but not lodging.[49]

Notes

A Well Documented Day

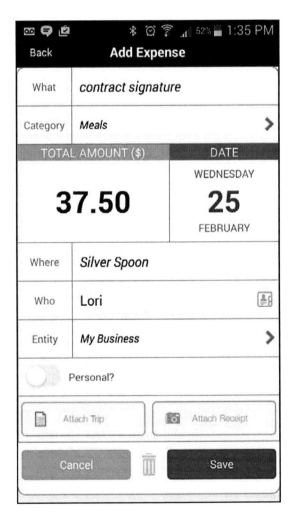

Strategy 14: Write it down properly and make it look neat.

General rule: The travel expense documentation rules are easily summarized: Either write down the expense properly on the day it happens or lose it. Congress continually reemphasizes that IRS is not to use or allow approximations of travel expenses.[50] Also, when you write it down neatly in a daily log, IRS spends much less time looking at your records.

Separate on the road expenses: You want your on the road expenses separated from your transportation expenses. On the road expenses are deductible for a business day.[51] Transportation expenses are deductible for a business trip.[52]

Documenting transportation expenses: When you are in business, you have two types of transportation: (1) local and (2) travel. Travel transportation takes place when you sleep away from home overnight. Travel transportation is also subject to one of the three tests that were explained earlier in the flowchart on page 40:

- 51/49 test

- 76/24 test

- Less than one week test

Important documentation needed for travel: To deduct travel expenses, your records must prove:[53]

- The amount you spent daily for such things as transportation, meals, and lodging

- The dates of your departure and return home from each trip, and the number of days spent on business while away from home

- Where you traveled, described by name of city, town, or similar designation

- Why you traveled, including the business reason for your travel or the business benefit derived or expected to be gained from the travel

Strategy 15: Keep a good tax diary. The Internal Revenue Code and IRS regulations require that travel expenditures be recorded at or near the time expenses are incurred.[54] IRS regulations state that contemporaneous records have a high degree of credibility not present with respect to a statement subsequent thereto when generally there is a lack of accurate recall.[55]

N

Notes

Travel Summary

Strategies to increase deductions:

1. Hire your spouse

2. Use business car for family travel

3. Drive 300 miles a day toward your business destination

4. Deduct dirty clothes

5. Take U.S. cruise ships

Strategies to lock in and increase amount of transportation deductions:

6. Make weekends deductible

7. Count travel days as deductible business days

8. Add pleasure to work days

Strategies that identify more reasons to travel for business with pleasure:

9. Look after your real estate

10. Visit colleagues

11. Get educated out of town

12. Hunt for a job

Strategies for audit proofing your travel deductions:

13. Keep the proper receipts

14. Write it down properly and make it look neat

15. Keep a good tax diary

Notes

Notes

3. Combine Personal Pleasure with Business Travel

1. U.S. v. Correll, 389 U.S. 299 (1967); Rev. Rul. 54-497, 1954-2 C.B. 75, superseded in part by Rev. Rul. 75-432, 1975-2 C.B. 60; Rev. Rul. 75-170, 1975-1 C.B. 60.

2. Ibid.

3. K. Waters, 12 T.C. 414, Dec. 16,873; C.M. Scott, (DC) 53-1 USTC & 9267, 110 F Supp 819.

4. H.O. Correll, (Sup. Ct.) 68-1 USTC & 9101, 389 U.S. 299.rev'g (CA-6) 66-2 USTC & 9778.

5. IRC 162(a)(2); 62(2)(B); Reg. § 1.162 -2(a), (b).

6. Ibid.

7. Ibid.

8. IRC 274(n)(1).

9. Section 1.274-5(c) of the Regulations; and IR 95-56, Notice 95-50, 1995-42 IRB.

10. Giordano v. Commissioner, 36 T.C.M. 430(1977); Howard v. Commissioner, 41 T.C.M. 1554(1981); Herder v. Commissioner, 38 T.C.M. 1244(1979); Rev. Rul. 55-57, 1955-1 C.B. 315; Lockwood v. Commissioner, 29 T.C.M. 618(1970). See also 274(m) of the Internal Revenue Code.

11. Regs 1.162-1(a); 1.162-2; IRC 162(a)(2).

12. Rev. Rul. 56-168, 1956-1 C.B. 93; Reg. § 1.162-2(c).

13. Ibid.

14. IRS Manual Handbook HB 1763 314(4).

15. Ibid, endnote 5. Also, Rev. Rul. 63-145, 1963-2 C.B. 86; T.R.-493, 7/24/63. Conference, 3/29/63.

16. IRC 274(h)(2).

17. Ibid.

18. Ibid.

19. IRC 274(h)(5).

20. Ibid.

21. IRC 274(c)(2)(B); 274(c)(1); Reg. § 1.274-4(d)(1); 1.162-2(b)(1).

22. Reg. § 1.274-4(d)(2)(v).

23. Reg. § 1.162-2(a)-(b)(1).

24. Reg. § 1.274-4(d)(2).

25. Reg. § 1.274-4(d)(2)(v).

26. Ibid.

27. Reg. § 1.162-2(b)(1)-(2); 1.274-4(d)(1).

28. Private Letter Ruling 9237014 as Reported in 4 Letter Ruling Review (No. 10) Pg. 4 (Oct. 1992).

29. Reg. § 1.274-4(d)(2)(i).

30. Ibid., IRS Pub. 463 (11/81) p.2; Your Federal Income Tax (11/81) p. 62.

31. Reg. § 1.274-4(d)(2)(i).

32. IRC 274(m)(1)(A).

33. Ibid.

34. Reg. § 5e.274-8h for travel after March 12, 1993.

35. Reg. § 1.274-4(d)(2)(ii).

36. Ibid.

37. Reg. § 1.274-4(d)(2)(iii); 1.162-2(b)(1).

38. Reg. § 1.274-4(d)(2)(iii).

39. Reg. § 1.274-4(d)(2)(iv).

40. IRC 162(a)(2).

41. IRS Publication 17, Your Federal Income Tax, as reproduced on page 142 of The Arthur Young Tax Guide,1989.

42. Ibid.

43. IRC 274(h)(1).

44. Rev. Rul. 75-120, 1975-1 CB 55.

45. IRC 274(d)(1).

46. Ibid.

47. Reg. § 1.274(c)(2)(iii)(a), (b).

48. Conference Report, p. II-27.

49. Rev Proc 2003-80, 2003-45 IRB 1037, Sec. 4.03, and Johnson, Marin I., (2000) 115 tc 210.

50. Conference Report, p. II-27.

51. Reg. § 162-2(a).

52. Reg. § 1.162-2(a).

53. IRC 274(d).

54. Reg. § 1.274-5(c)(1).

55. Ibid.

Notes

4 Hire and Lease from Relatives

Overview: Since inception of the income tax, tax advisors have been developing techniques to shift income within family groups. Some basic principles are well defined. Others have been totally altered by various tax reforms.

Strategies for Employing Your Spouse in Your Schedule C Business

Strategy 1: Set the stage for your spouse's fringe benefits by employing your spouse in your sole proprietorship, but paying the minimum wage.

Wages subject to social security taxes: Wages paid by husband to wife and by wife to husband are subject to Social Security.[1]

Pay lowest reasonable wage: There's no benefit in trying to qualify for extra social security retirement monies by paying extra social security taxes; accordingly, pay your spouse as little as legally possible. IRS takes the position that wages must be reasonable for the job performed. Structure this with your accountant to pay the lowest reasonable wage possible. See page 65 for reasonable wage factors.

Bona fide employment: The employment of your spouse must be bona fide.[2] IRS will, as it should, start by questioning whether or not your spouse did any work at all. You must have evidence of actual work done for this deduction to stand IRS scrutiny.

Strategy 2: Take advantage of your spouse's employment with a plan to pay the medical expenses of your employees and their families.

Pay for insurance: You, as a sole proprietor business, can pay for medical insurance to cover your employees and their families if they *legitimately* work in the business. The deduction is 100% starting in 2003. S Corporations cannot deduct medical premiums for stockholders who own 2% or more of the corporation. However, the medical premiums incurred by S Corporations are deductible on the individual owner's tax return as an adjustment to income.

Limitations: The deductibility of medical insurance premiums for self-employed tax payers does have limitations. The first is that it is limited to your net income from your business or to the earned income from the business that pays the medical insurance. Thus, if you have a loss, you won't be able to deduct the premiums. Secondly, you cannot deduct any premiums if you were covered in part by a subsidized employer's plan. Thus, if your employer pays 50% of the premiums and you pay the other 50%, you cannot deduct the portion that you pay as an adjustment for gross income. You may be able to deduct your portion as an itemized deduction.

Note: As a result of ObamaCare, if you have employees covered under a Self Insured Medical Plan, you will need to also pay for medical insurance or there could be a penalty.

Pay for coinsurance and deductible: You could design the plan to cover coinsurance and deductible for those employees who are covered by plans other than the one you provide, and for other expenses that are not covered by insurance (i.e. over the counter medications).

2014=

2015 HSA Limits	Self Only	Family
Minimum Deductible	$1,300	$2,600
Annual Out-Of-Pocket	$6,450	$12,900
Maximum Contribution	$3,350	$6,650
Catch-Up Contribution	$1,000	$1,000 each

#1.) Either Hire your Spouse/family Members
in a Self Employed Business on a Regular C Corp. (only)

#2.) Draft up a Self Medical Reimbursement PLAN.
(see Tax Lawyer $700 fee) Tax Deductable

#3) Whoever family - they Are the Primary Insurer.
Individual contracts

#4) Either a C Corp or Hire Spouse in Self Employed Business
"Elect family Coverage 4 Children under 26.

#5) Reimburse Medical Exp. for family members. that are
Not Covered by Insurance.
EXP.> CO-PAY

#6) Met w/ Accountant to Make Sure the payments under
the Self Insure payments Plans are Reasonable

* Non discrimination P.59

100% reimbursement of medical expenses: You can design your medical plan to reimburse employees for every penny of otherwise deductible medical expense. Some could be paid by insurance and some directly by the proprietorship. It must, however, be nondiscriminatory and you should keep the plan in force for at least 3 years.[3A] Be sure to keep receipts for all medical expenses that will be reimbursed.[3B]

Note: Based on what appears to be the position of the IRS on audits, the total wages and potential payout of the Self Insured Medical Reimbursement Plan must constitute a reasonable wage for the hours worked. Thus, you need to put a dollar limit on the yearly payout that the plan will produce. Have your accountant or financial planner evaluate the maximum limits possible under the plan so yo don't exceed reasonable compensation.

Nondiscrimination required of medical reimbursement: A self-insured medical reimbursement plan must not discriminate in favor of the owners or highly compensated employees. In addition, it must cover all full-time employees. Despite the above, the IRS allows some safe harbor discrimination as follows:

- Routine physical for employees
- Anyone who works less than 25 hours per week
- Anyone under the age of 25
- Anyone who ordinarily works less than seven months per year
- Anyone who has less than three years of service

Revenue rule: In Revenue Ruling 71-588 and in the ISP Coordinated Issue Paper, IRS ruled that amounts reimbursed under an accident and health plan covering all bona fide employees, including the owner's spouse and family, may not be included in the employee/spouse's gross income and are deductible by the owner as business expenses. Moreover, in a Technical Advice Memorandum, IRS allowed a self-employed individual to hire his/her spouse and elect family coverage under a self insured medical reimbursement plan.[4]

One employee only: IRS Reg. 1.105-5 states that a medical reimbursement plan can have as few as one employee. Thus, if your only employee is your spouse, you can still qualify for a medical reimbursement plan if you legitimately hire your spouse in your business.

Like a corporation: A similar rule applies to corporations and some Schedule C taxpayers form corporations to obtain tax-deductible medical coverage at the corporate level.

Overview of HSA's: An HSA requires a trust to be set up for paying qualified medical expenses. The contributions are deductible, and the payments for qualified medical expenses are tax-free. *HEALTH SAVINGS ACCT.*

Qualifying: You must use the HSA proceeds for qualified medical expenses. In addition, you must have a high deductible medical policy.[4A] The deductible requirements and contribution limits are indicated on the left hand page. Also, there are catch-up contributions allowed for those who are age 55 or older

Observation: In my opinion, the Self Insured Medical Reimbursement Plan is still the better option since you don't need a high deductible policy, don't need to set up a trust with yearly fees paid to financial institutions, and it doesn't have any dollar limitations on contributions (other than the fact that the payments must be reasonable for the hours and work performed). An HSA, however, might be advisable if you are single and don't have a C corporation or you don't want to hire your spouse in your business in order to utilize the benefits of the Self Insured Medical Reimbursement Plan.

Caution: You can't have another medical plan that covers your deductibles. Thus, if you have a plan such as AFLAC that pays for sickness and injuries, this may disqualify your HSA. However, you can have a plan that pays for specific types of diseases such as Cancer, and you can have a plan that pays for daily stays in hospitals. In addition, you can have both a Self Insured Medical Plan, Flexible Spending Account or Cafeteria Plan in addition to the HSA IF these plans have at least the same deductibles as the HSA.

Flowchart for Determining If You Can Benefit From the Supper Money Tax Strategy

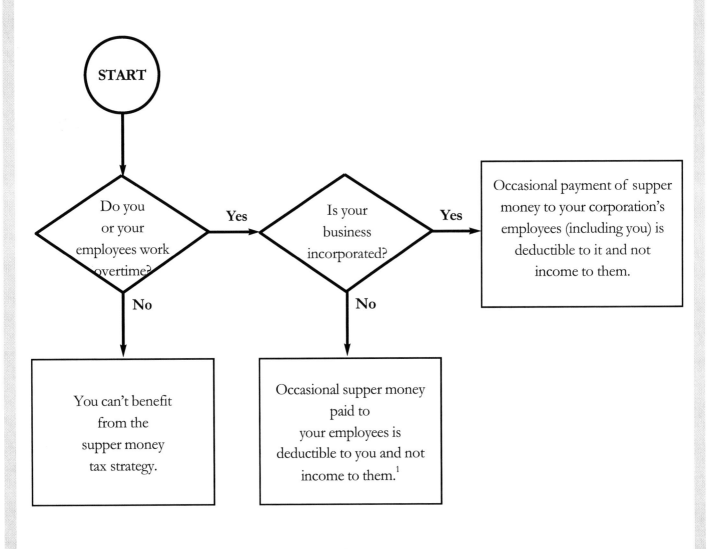

START

Do you or your employees work overtime?

Yes → Is your business incorporated?

Yes → Occasional payment of supper money to your corporation's employees (including you) is deductible to it and not income to them.

No → You can't benefit from the supper money tax strategy.

No → Occasional supper money paid to your employees is deductible to you and not income to them.[1]

Sole Owner
401K Profit Sharing Plan
— 100% of what you Make up to $18K
+20% if inc
or Self Emp

[1]You cannot exclude supper money you pay to yourself. See <u>Antos v. Commissioner</u>, 35 TCM (CCH) 387 (1976), aff'd by 9th Cir in unpub. opinion dated 2/24/78.

Strategy 3: Establish an educational benefit program for employees.

Deductible expenses: Just as you can for yourself, you may deduct the ordinary and necessary expenses you pay for the education and training of your employees.[5] The deductible payments include books, tuition, fees, travel, transportation, lodging, and other expenses necessary to obtain the education.[6] See also Appendix F for Hope scholarship credits, lifetime learning credits, and student loan interest deductions.

Education deduction rule: The education of your employee/spouse must be related to your employee's current job.[7] It must improve or maintain the skills of your employee.[8] To ensure deductibility, the courses should not end in an undergraduate degree.[9] Also, the courses should not qualify your employee/spouse for a new trade or profession.[10]

Strategy 4: Establish a supper money allowance for hard-working employees.

Proprietor not eligible: As a Schedule C taxpayer, you are not eligible for supper money.

Employees are eligible: Meals and lodging provided by you to an employee, for your convenience as an employer, are deducted by you on Schedule C and are not considered income to your employee (spouse).[11] Tax law allows deductions for supper, taxi fare, and other personal expenses when employees work late due to extraordinary demands of the business that are occasional and enable the employee to work overtime.[12]

Example: You pay $20 as a supper allowance whenever an employee works more than 10 hours and one minute during a workday. Jackson works 12 such days during the year. Jackson receives $240.00 and you deduct $240.00. This would be 100% deductible.

Flowchart: Review the flowchart on the page on left for those eligible for the supper money allowance.

Strategy 5: Set up a qualified plan and IRA Without question, if I had to pick the best strategy that you can do to reduce your taxes, I would recommend setting up a qualified SEP, Simple IRA, Roth IRA and an Education IRA, or profit sharing plan. The type of plan that best suits you will vary depending on your income and if you have employees. Following are our recommendations:

1. If you have two or more non-family employees: Set up a simple IRA. This allows you to contribute 100% of your net income or wages (if incorporated) up to $12,500 in 2015, plus a catch up contribution of $3,000 if you are age 50 or over. In addition, the company can match the contribution up to 3% of wages. The key is that the employee contributes most of the money and not you, the self-employed owner. If the employee makes no contribution, you are not obligated to contribute anything since you only need to match their contribution up to a maximum of 3% of their wages.

Alternative: As an alternative to the Simple IRA, you might want to consider an "age weighted" profit sharing plan. If you are substantially older than your staff, you might be able to contribute substantially more for you than what would be required for your staff, which means more money in your pocket. I have seen as much as 20% of the net income for the older owner (up to the yearly $53,000 maximum in 2015) and much less (3% of wages) for younger workers. The only drawback is that the plan requires an Actuary which costs several thousand dollars each year.

2. If you have no non-family employees and earn under $200,000 net income per year: We would recommend a combination sole owner 401(k) and a profit sharing plan. This allows you to contribute up to $18,000 in 2015 to the 401(k) AND another 20% of your income to the profit sharing plan.

3. You have no non-family employees and earn over $200,000 of net income per year: We would recommend a SEP.

Note: The total contributions to both plans are limited to $53,000 in 2015 (unless you are age 50 or over).

61

Notes

50 OVER
2015 CATCH-UP -
IRA — 1000

Spouse / Children
- Contracts
- Time Sheet
- Pay by Check

SEPs: A SEP[13] is easy and cheap to maintain. You can put in up to 20% of your net earnings with a maximum of $53,000 for 2015. In addition, you can choose to contribute as much or as little for each year, which gives a great deal of flexibility. For corporations, you can deduct 25% of all wages. Thus, corporations get a slightly higher deduction percentage.

Tip: If you cover at least one other non-highly compensated employee, you can get a tax credit of 50% of your administrative costs up to a maximum credit of $500.[14]

Roth IRAs: In 2015, you can put away $5,500[15] into either a deductible IRA or a non-deductible Roth IRA. However, if the money is used for retirement, education for your family, or for a first time homebuyer, the distribution is completely tax-free.[16] This is much better than the traditional IRA, but starts phasing out for single taxpayers whose adjusted gross income is over $116,000-$131,000, and $183,000-$193,000 for joint filers.[17]

Note: You can convert your regular IRA, SEP, or most qualified pension and profit sharing plans to a Roth IRA with no income limitations in 2013 and thereafter.[18] Beware that some states may provide penalties for the rollover in computing their state income tax.

Strategy 5A: Catch up contributions of an extra $1,000 for traditional and Roth IRA's, $3,000 for Simple IRA's, and $6,000 for SEP's and other qualified plans are available if you are age 50 or older in 2015.[19]

Strategy 5B: Don't forget the saver's tax credit, which could be as much as 50% of the first $2,000 of pension or IRA contributions for you and your spouse.[20] However, the catch is that you must earn less than the following AGI in 2015:

2015						
Joint Return		**Head of Household**		**Married Filing Separate**		**Applicable Percentage**
Over	Not Over	Over	Not Over	Over	Not Over	
0	$36,500	0	$27,375	0	$18,250	50%
$36,500	$39,500	$27,375	$29,625	$18,250	$19,750	20%
$39,500	$61,000	$29,625	$45,750	$19,750	$30,500	10%
$61,000	-	$45,750	-	$30,500	-	0%

Example: Sam and Jane each contribute $2,000 to an IRA for a total of $4,000. Their AGI is under $36,500, so their maximum credit is $2,000 (50% of each contribution).[21]

Strategy For Schedule C Parents With Children Age 7 Through 17: Hiring Children

Strategy 6: First $6,300 is tax-free to child: In 2015, the standard deduction is $6,300[22] and the dependency exemption is $4,000.[23] Therefore, the first $6,300 is tax-free to child and zero if claimed as a dependent by another.[24] They then pay tax on the first $9,225 in taxable income at the 10% tax rate.[25]

Example: You pay your child $6,300 in wages for the year 2015. You can deduct $6,300 in reasonable wages on your schedule C (Schedule E if in connection with rental properties). You pay no social security or unemployment taxes (if they are under age 18). Your child reports the $6,300 as income from wages on IRS form 1040 and then deducts $6,300 as his or her standard deduction.

Subsidy: If you are in the 35% bracket, the $6,300 produces a tax refund/savings of $2,205 from federal taxes plus potential savings of $182 from Medicare surcharge. Above $6,300, you save at a 25% rate (35% - 10%).

Dependent Child's Business Services and Wage Sheet

Time Billing

Month: July   Employee: I.M. Child

Date	Activity	Hours Worked
Monday, 7th	Sorted files & made 3x5 cards	4
Tues, 8th	Cleaned office & emptied trash	2
Thurs, 10th	Addressed brochures	2
Sat, 12th	Arranged business trip files	2
"	Typed business letter	2
	Total Hours Worked	12
	Times Hourly Wage	$5.00
	Total Wages Due	$60.00

All relatives must perform some real work to be able to hire them and deduct their wages: I had a friend who hired his children in his business to be a janitor in his manufacturing plant during the summers. All wages were paid by check. He kept time sheets and the wages were reasonable. When the IRS agent, who was auditing him, wanted to go to the bathroom, the children didn't know where the bathroom was, and note, they were the janitors! In short, if you are going to hire your children or spouse, always show them where the bathrooms are. Secondly, if they don't legitimately work in your business, you can't pay them a deductible wage. It's that simple.

Perspective: In effect, Uncle Sam underwrites the education, weddings, and other uses to which your children put their money.

Why age 7 and over: The "age 7 and over" comes from the Eller case in which Eller hired his three children, including the youngest who was age 7. IRS contested the employment of the 7-year-old, but lost in court. Recently IRS acquiesced to (agreed to follow) the Eller case effectively approving employment of 7- year-olds.[26]

Setting your child's salary: Unlike your spouse, you want to pay your child as much as possible because there's no payroll tax penalty on the wages. The salary or wage you pay must be reasonable to be deductible.[27] This means that the amount you pay for services must be similar to amounts paid for similar services by similar businesses under similar circumstances.[28] When setting the salary, be sure to allow for the experience (or inexperience) and ability of your child. Also, consider the 10 factors IRS uses to examine wages for reasonableness:[29]

- Duties performed
- Volume of work
- Type and amount of responsibility
- Complexity of work
- Amount of time required for work
- General cost of living in the area
- Ability and achievements of the employee
- Comparison of amount of salary with amount of business income
- Your pay policy regarding all employees (if there are others)
- Pay history of the employee

Documentation Strategies To Follow When Employing Your Spouse And Children In Your Schedule C Business

Strategy 7: Require a weekly time sheet. If you were an IRS auditor, would you believe that your child or spouse was a bonafide employee? You would only if you saw adequate proof. In most cases, it's absolutely essential that your relatives fill out a time sheet at the end of each week. To get your deductions for wages, you must be able to prove what work was actually performed.[30] Each day that your relative works, the time sheet should show:

- Date
- Description of tasks performed
- Hours worked

Notes

2015 RATE
CAPITAL GAINS
15 — 23.8%
UPTO
& 74,899 Married filed jointly
∅ RATE for earnings under.

GIFT TAX

Strategy 8: Pay by check. At the end of each day or week, you should approve the time sheet. Payment to your spouse or child should always be made by check. Even if your child is too you.. checking account, you should pay by check. In this circumstance, establish a custodial checking your local bank. The check completes the audit trail by establishing (1) that you paid the child a.. the child actually received the payment.

Strategy 9: File the proper IRS forms.

The first step to hiring employees, relatives or others, is to obtain a taxpayer ID number from IRS. Next, make sure you complete the necessary payroll paperwork. There's paperwork even on your under age 18 child who, as the employee of parents, is exempt from Social Security and unemployment taxes.[31] However, even if no taxes are due, you must complete the following paperwork:

- **IRS Form W-4.** This simple form must be completed by your employees and stored in your files.[32]

- **IRS Form W-2.** If you pay your spouse or child any amount and withhold taxes, you must give your employees a copy of IRS Form W-2 and file it along with IRS Form W-3 with both IRS and the Social Security Administration.[33]

- **IRS Form 1099.** If you pay wages of $600 or more and do not withhold taxes, you must give the recipient a 1099 and report the wages to the IRS (corporate recipients are exempt from 1099).

- **IRS Form 941.** Use this form quarterly to report withheld income taxes and deposits.[34]

- **IRS Form 940.** Although you are not liable for unemployment taxes on wages paid to your child, if your child is a dependent and under age 21, you must file IRS Form 940 at the end of the year.[35] If your child is your only employee, you simply enter your child's wages as exempt from unemployment tax and return the form to IRS.[36]

- **IRS Form SS4.** Employer ID Number.

You will need your child's social security number to complete the payroll paperwork. The social security number should be obtained when the child is born.

Forms can be downloaded directly from the IRS at <u>www.irs.gov</u> by clicking on "Forms & Publications".

Strategy 10: Get an employment contract.

Have your lawyer draft an employment contract noting pay rate, duties, benefits, etc. Pay should be based on hours worked.[37]

Strategies For Those Whose Children Are Age Inappropriate, Those Who Just Do Not Want To Employ Their Children, And Those Who Want To Move Money To Friends

Strategy 11: Use gifts of property to push taxes to your lower bracket relatives age 18 and over and friends.

Overview: With this strategy, you gift property rather than cash to a person in a lower tax bracket. The lower bracket person sells the property and pays the tax.

Note: People in the 10% - 15% tax brackets (single earners under $37,450 taxable income or married filing jointly under $74,900 in taxable income) pay zero federal capital gains tax in 2015. However, this income limit includes any capital gains, net of capital and business losses.

Notes

Result: The unit (donor and donee) has more cash to spend because Uncle Sam took less tax from the person in the lower tax bracket.

Gift tax rule for singles: In 2015, you can give away $14,000 each year to as many people as you want without having to worry about any tax rules.[38] You don't get a tax deduction for the gift but the recipient doesn't have taxable income.[39] It is a free move of your money or assets. This amount will become indexed to inflation.

Gift tax rule for married: If you are married, you and your spouse together can give up to $28,000 to any number of persons without incurring a gift tax.[40] However, when gifts to one individual exceed the $14,000 threshold, husband and wife must agree that it's a joint gift and a gift tax return must be filed.[41] For gifts of $14,000 or less, no gift tax return needs to be filed.[42] I should note that there is also a five million dollar lifetime gift tax exclusion in addition to the yearly exclusions for gifts.

Value of the gift: For gift tax purposes, the value of the gift is equal to the property's fair market value at the date the property is transferred.[43]

Basis for income tax calculations: The recipient's tax basis of the gift for income tax purposes is equal to your basis. If you transfer a fully depreciated car, the recipient's basis for purposes of computing depreciation is zero.[44] It's also zero for purposes of computing gain or loss on sale.[45]

Example facts: You paid $20,000 for a car that's been used 75% of the time for business and is fully depreciated for tax purposes. You hate the car and are looking forward to selling it on the open market for $8,000. You are in the 35% bracket and your 21-year-old son is in the 10% bracket.

If you sell: Since the car is fully depreciated, all of the $6,000 business proceeds (75% x $8,000) are taxed at your 35% tax bracket for a tax of $2,100. You also have a personal non-deductible loss on the undepreciated 25% personal portion of the car.

If son sells: You transfer title to your son. Under the gift tax rules, he steps in your shoes and pays a tax of only $0 in his tax bracket, the family unit saves $2,100.

Notes

Why age 24 and over: Starting in 2008 and thereafter, Congress has passed a Kiddie Tax which is applicable to investment income. In 2015, children under age 24 can only earn up to $2,100 of investment income; the first $1,050 is tax free and the next $1,050 is taxed at the child's tax bracket.[46] Anything above $2,100 is taxed at the parent's tax bracket. The Kiddie tax applies to any child under age 24 who is a full time student, unless they are married filing a joint return, or their earned income is over 50% of their total support; in this case it's under age 18.

Observation: Although Congress did try to limit the benefits of the "gift lease back" and "gifts to push tax" techniques, you can still shift $2,100, per kid each year, of investment income and have it taxed to the child at their tax brackct.

Strategy 12: Create deductions by gifting property to lower tax bracket friends and relatives age 18 and over and then leasing the property back for business use.

Step 1: Gift the property. To put the gift/leaseback strategy to work, you must first own the asset. You, as an individual, may gift assets to your children or any other persons.[48] Your corporation may not make such gifts.[49]

Step 2: Gift the right property. Fully depreciated property produces the maximum deductions for the gift/leaseback strategy. By using fully depreciated assets in a gift/leaseback, you actually create new deductions. Fully depreciated assets produce no depreciation deductions. However, the gift/leaseback technique creates a new rent reduction from the fully depreciated equipment.

Example: You own and use in your business a Chevrolet Caprice Classic. The car is fully depreciated. It has a retail value of $8,425, as published by the National Automobile Dealers Association in its Used Car Guide. According to IRS's Official Annual Lease Value Table, the annual rent on the Caprice should be $2,600 for the next four years.[50] You gift and transfer the car's title to a trust established for your 18-year-old daughter.

Results: You get a tax deduction for the $2,600 rent you pay to the trust each year.[51] Assuming you were in the 46.5% tax bracket for the state and Federal purposes, your taxes are reduced by $1,209. Your 18-year-old daughter received $2,600 from the trust and paid a tax of $196. The family unit — you and your daughter — received a net tax benefit of $1,013 from a car that otherwise would have produced no tax benefit.

Give away property you need to use today but don't want five years from now: When you give property away, it's no longer yours. Therefore, give away personal property that's declining in value daily, such as cars, computers, photocopier, etc.

Who would be an eligible recipient of the leaseback? Anyone whom you would give money to anyway. You can do this with spouses, kids, parents, siblings, and significant friends. In short, anyone!

Minors: If you make a gift to a minor, you may have to use a trust to make things proper. If you put property in a trust and that trust will return the property to you, you are taxed on the income of the trust. It is important that an independent trustee be used for all trusts and that the trust corpus and income must not return to you.[52]

Document fair values: You must have evidence to support both fair market value and fair rental charges. With automobiles, use the Blue Book for fair values and IRS tables or evidence from commercial leasing companies for fair rental values. With photocopier, desks, chairs, and similar assets, contact commercial leasing companies. Have them prepare a formal document estimating values. Finally, make sure that all terms of the lease are in writing (standard forms are available in office supply stores).

Notes

Strategy 13: Lease business assets purchased by your lower bracketed friends and relatives age 18 and over: You can gift money to your friends and relatives. It's now their money and they can use it as they please. They can buy cars, computers, etc., and set up a leasing business.

Strategy 14: Set up a Section 529 plan for kids: You can set aside up to several hundred thousand dollars for each kid's education. The funds can be used for any relative, and the appreciation is tax free if used for college and graduate school tuition and.[53]

These funds can be used for any qualified higher education expenses such as tuition, required fees, and supplies and books.[54] It can also be used for reasonable costs for room and board if the student is in residence for at least half time.[55] Now they can also be used to buy a computer and internet access for the student.[55A]

Finally, the contribution to any prepaid tuition or Section 529 Plan qualifies for the annual gift tax yearly exclusion (i.e. $14,000 per donee if you are a single taxpayer or $28,000 if you are married taxpayers filing a joint return in 2015). However, when gifts to one individual exceed the $14,000 threshold, husband and wife must agree that it's a joint gift and a gift tax return must be filed.[41] For gifts of $14,000 or less, no gift tax return needs to be filed.[42]

Strategy 15: Sell assets to and lease assets back from lower bracket friends and relatives age 18 and over. This technique, known as a sale and leaseback, has been around for years. It puts the friend or relative in the leasing business, but allows you to select the asset.

Example: You sell your house at fair market value to your son using installment notes. Your son leases the house back to you at fair market rent.

Result: You and your son have almost even cash flow, but your son now has passive losses from the rental property.

Get a good lawyer: The techniques noted in strategies 10-14 must be done correctly.[56] The lease should be for a short term and definitely not exceed the seller's life expectancy. The rent and sale price should be at fair market value. All payments should be made to the appropriate parties. No forgiveness of any payment should occur, especially in the first two years.

Document non-tax business reason: In addition, many courts[57] require a non-tax reason for a sale-lease-back or gift-leaseback. A letter from a lawyer stating that this transaction is recommended for:

- Protection from creditors
- Avoidance of ethical conflicts
- Provisions for professional management
- Avoidance of problems with shareholders and/or business associates
- Avoidance of estate tax and probate

You should have a valid business purpose for each step in the transaction.[58] In addition, the owner/lessor must acquire and retain "significant and genuine attributes" of a traditional owner including the benefits and burdens of ownership. See your lawyer or tax advisor about this.

Notes

Hire And Lease Summary

Strategies for employing spouse in Schedule C Business

1. Set the stage for fringe benefits by hiring your spouse; however, pay the minimum wage

2. Establish a medical plan to cover your employee / spouse and family

3. Establish educational benefit plan

4. Establish supper money allowance

5. Set up a simple savings plan

Strategy for Schedule C parents with children age 7 - 17

6. Employ dependent children age 7 and over but under age 18

Documentation strategies to follow when employing your spouse and children in your Schedule C business

7. Require a weekly time sheet

8. Pay by check

9. File proper IRS forms

Strategies for those whose children are age inappropriate, those who just do not want to employ their children, and those who want to move money to friends

10. Get an employment contract

11. Gift and have a relative or friend sell

12. Gift and lease back the gifted property

13. Give money and lease assets with the money

14. Set up Section 529 Plan for kids

15. Sell and lease back

Notes

4. Hire And Lease From Your Relatives

1. IRC §§ 3121(b)(3)(A); 3306(c)(5). See also I.R.S. Pub. Circular E.
2. Reg. § 1.162-7(a).
3. IRS Letter Ruling 9409006, ISP Coordinated Issue Paper (UIC-162.35.22).
3A. Francis vs. Commissioner, TC Memo 2007-33 (2/8/2007).
3B. Alverez vs. Commissioner: T.C. memo 2007-144
4. Rev. Rul. 2003-102, 2003-38 IRB 448 & Peter Speltz vs. Comm; T.C. Summary Opinion 2006-25.
4A. Section 223(c)(1)(A) of the IRC. Rev Proc 2012-26 & 2013-25
4B. Section 223(c)(1)(A) of the IRC and Rev. Proc. 2010-22.
4C. Section 223(g) of the IRC and Rev. Proc. 2010-22 & Rev Proc 2012-32, 2012-22 IRB
5. Reg. § 1.162-5; Rev. Rul., 76-71, 1976-1 C.B. 308.
6. IRS Pub. 508 (Rev. Nov. 85) p. 2.
7. Rev. Rul. 76-71, 1976-1 C.B. 308.
8. Reg. § 1.162-5(a)(1).
9. Reg. § 1.162-5(b)(2).
10. Reg. § 1.162-5(b)(3).
11. IRC. § 119(a); Reg. § 1.119-1; Rev. Rul. 71-411, 1971-2 C.B. 103; Rev. Rul. 71-267, 1971-1 C.B. 37.
12. IRC. § 132(a)(4); IRS Pub. 535 (Rev. Dec. 85) p. 15. § 132-6 of the Regulations.
13. § 408(k)(6)(D) of the Internal Revenue Code.
14. § 45(E) of the Internal Revenue Code.
15. § 408(A)(c)(1) of the Internal Revenue Code.
16. § 219 of the Internal Revenue Code.
17. § 408(c)(3)(C) of the Internal Revenue Code.
18. IRS Notice 2009-75, Sect III Q&A 2(a), 2009-39 IRB 436.
19. § 414(v) of the Internal Revenue Code.
20. § 25(b) of the Internal Revenue Code.
21. § 25(b)(1)(A) of the Internal Revenue Code.
22. Revenue Procedure 2013-15
23. IRC § 151(d)(1)(A); IBID. See *"Federal Tax Expert"*, Kleinrock Publishing.
24. IRC § 151(d)(2).
25. IRC § 1(h)(2)(C).
26. 77 T.C. 934; A. 1984-2 C.B. 1.
27. IRC § 162(a)(1).
28. Reg. § 1.162-7(b)(3).
29. IRS Pub. 535 (Rev. 2001) p.4
30. Reg. § 1.162-7(a).
31. IRC §§ 3121(b)(3)(A), 3306(c)(5).

32. Reg. § 31.3402(n)-1(b).

33. IRS Instructions For Preparing Forms W-2, W-3.37.

34. Reg. § 31.3402(n)-1; IRS Instructions For Preparing Form 941.

35. IRS Instructions for Preparing Form 940.

36. Ibid.

37. Haeder; TC Memo 2000-7.

38. IRC § 2503(b). See Rev. Proc. 2007-66, 2007-45 IRB 970.

39. IRC § § 274(b)(1); 102(a).

40. IRC § 2513(a); Reg. § 25.2513-1(c).

41. IRC § § 6019; 2503(b); Reg. § 25.2513-1(c).

42. Ibid.

43. IRC § 2512(a); Reg. § 25.2513-1(c).

44. IRC § 1015(a).

45. Reg. § 1.1015-1(a)(1).

46. IRC § 1(i). Rev. Proc. 2001-59, 2001-52 I.R.B. pg 623

47. IRS Form 8615, Computation of Tax for Children Under Age 14 Who Have Investment Income of More than $1,500 (2001); Rev. Proc. 2001-59 IRB; pg 623
   IRC § 1(i)(4)(A).

48. IRC § 2503(b).

49. E.g., Epstein v. Commissioner, 53 T.C. 459 (1969), acq. 1970-2 C.B. 19.

50. Reg. § 1.61-2T(d)(2)(iii).

51. IRC § 162(a)(3).

52. IRC § 673 (a).

53. IRC § 529 (c)(3)(B).

54. IRC § 529 (e)(5).

55A. Amended IRC § 529 (e)(3)(A) by 2009 Recover Act Section 1005(a)

55. IRC § 529 (e)(3)(B).

56. Estate of Maxwell, 98 TC 39 (1992).

57. Matthews vs. Comm., 61 T.C. 12 (1973), rev'd 75-2 U.S. T.C. Par 967 (5th 1975) and Frank Lyons Co. vs. Comm. 435 U.S. 561 (S Ct. 1978).

58. IRS Notice 2005-13.

Notes

5 Get Your Maximum Business Automobile Deductions

Overview: Tax rules applicable to the business automobile have become so complex that this entire seminar could be devoted to cars only. Since that's not the plan, this section of the seminar will concentrate on ways to not only increase your deductions, but also lock them in with proper documentation tactics.

Strategies to Increase Your Daily Deductions

Strategy 1: Use two cars for business to get maximum deductions.

Rationale: If you drive only one car for business, what's the maximum business use percentage you can achieve? That's right: 100 percent. If you drive two cars for business, could you drive one car 100 percent for business and the other car 100 percent for business? Yes![1] Your business use is based on business miles driven.

Calculation: You figure business use by dividing business miles by total miles driven.[2] You do this for each car driven for business.[3]

How The Two Car Strategy Produces Extra Deductions

Homewood Accountant
CH 40 2013 Tax Return

	One Car *(Chrysler)*	Two Cars Car 1 *(Honda)*	Car 2 *(BMW)*
Business/Personal Use			
Total Mileage for Business	22,000	18,000	4,000
Total Mileage for Year	24,000	20,000	7,800
Business Use Percentage	**92%**	**90%**	**51%**
Deduction Calculations			
Gas and Oil	$4,992	$4,160	$1,622
Insurance	$1,200	$1,200	$1,000
Repairs and Maintenance	$1,200	$1,200	$1,200
Tags and Licenses	$150	$150	$150
Wash and Wax	$230	$230	$230
Other	$50	$50	$50
Total Operating Expense	$7,822	$6,990	$4,252
Business Use Percentage	x 92%	x 90%	x 51%
Business Total	$7,196	$6,291	$2,169
Depreciation	$5,152	$5,040	$2,800
Total Deductions	$12,348	$11,331	$4,969
Extra Deductions		$3,952	

Note: The cars in this example cost $28,000 each and are new.

Interest, state and local taxes are also deductible under both the IRS and actual methods to the extent ⁞e automobile is used for business. Rev. Proc. 2010-51.

Strategy 2: Convert personal cars to business use to increase your spendable cash.

Don't buy a second car: The two car strategy puts extra money in your pocket only when you are converting an otherwise personal asset to business use. In other words, if you have two cars in your family, make them both deductible, but don't buy a second car to implement the two car strategy.

Caution: One disadvantage of using two cars in a business or bringing another car into your business during the year is that you must keep track of your mileage on a daily basis. The simplifying techniques mentioned on page 93 cannot be used.

What to depreciate: [4] You are allowed to depreciate the basis of your car. Because the car was used for personal purposes, you determine basis on the day you convert the car to business use. On that day, you determine basis by comparing cost and market value of the car and using the lower of the two.[5] Accountants call this the lower of cost or market value rule.

What cost is: As used here, cost is what you paid for the car originally plus capital improvements such as amounts spent to rebuild or replace an engine.[6]

What market value is: Market value is the fair market value of the automobile on the day you convert it to business use.[7] Generally, you can determine market value by referring to the Blue Book. All financial institutions and automobile dealerships subscribe to the Blue Book: *The National Automobile Dealer's Association Official Used Car Guide*. The Blue Book lists two values for used cars: (1) retail and (2) wholesale. Since you will use the Blue Book's value for determining depreciation, you want the higher number — the retail price. That's what you would have to pay to purchase the car and what a regular customer would have to pay to a dealer. It's also the number that gives you the most depreciation.

Example: Assume you purchased your personal car several years ago for $8,000. Today, that car has a retail book value of $5,000. Your basis for purposes of computing depreciation is $5,000 (the lower of cost or fair market value.)[8]

Notes

Bmw
Acct - Amended file Fed / State returns
Business use of Bmw
up to last 2-3 yrs of
Business -

- 2015 -
★ Business 57.5¢
Charitable - 14.¢
Medical/Move 23¢

★ 24¢ Depreciation

Older Car -
Cheaper the car
Better value Tax
wise - get 57.5¢
per Mile

How to Find the Largest Deduction
for Your Automobile

	One Car	Two Cars		Two Cars
		Car 1	Car 2	
Actual Cents per Mile*				
Total Deductions	$12,348	$11,331	$4,969	$16,300
Business Miles	÷22,000	÷18,000	÷4,000	÷22,000
Cents per Mile	.56	.63	1.24	.74
Deductions with IRS Rates				
Business Miles	22,000	18,000	4,000	22,000
Cents per Mile	x .575	x .575	x .575	x .575
Total Deductions	$12,650	$10,350	$2,300	$12,650
Savings Calculation				
IRS Rate Deductions	$12,650	$10,350	$2,300	$12,650
Actual Expense Deductions	-12,348	-11,331	-4,969	-16,330
Benefit (Detriment)	$302	($981)	($2,669)	($3,680)

*See page 80 for actual expense calculations.

Strategy 3: Deduct the larger of the actual expense deduction or the IRS optional mileage rate deduction.

Who can use IRS rates: Unlike corporations, individuals such as the self-employed have a choice: Use either IRS optional mileage rates or the actual expenses to deduct business automobile expenses.

2015 rates: The 2015 IRS optional mileage rates are:[9]

- 57.5 cents for business miles
- 14 cents for charitable activities
- 23 cents for medical and moving

The new rules are straightforward: The 2015 rate applies to all business miles[12]. There is no 15,000 annual limit and no maximum.

Example: In 2015, you drive 20,000 Miles @ 57.5 cents = Total Deduction $11,500

Depreciation built into the rates: The 2015 IRS standard mileage rate has a depreciation component built into the rates;[13]

- 24 cents for depreciation
- 33.5 cents for operating expenses

Depreciation: Each 57.5 cents per mile deduction reduces the basis of your business car by 24 cents. Thus, if you drove 20,000 miles, your depreciation for the year would be $4,800 and that reduces your basis by that amount, but not below zero.[14]

Switch to actual allowed: If you currently use IRS rates, you may switch to actual.[15]

Switch to IRS mileage rate: Generally, you may not switch from the actual method to the IRS allowance unless straight line depreciation was used.[16]

Strategy 4: Select the fastest depreciation method to obtain maximum annual deductions: Depreciation is nothing more than a cost allocation method; therefore, pick the method that gives you the largest deductions each year.

Tax Leasing Advantages

Leasing is good if you meet a few of the underlying criteria:

(1)   Your financial income does not vary from year to year.

(2)   It is important to drive a new vehicle in your business.

(3)   You don't like to own cars for many years.

(4)   You generally drive less than 15,000 miles per year, and keep it for three years or less.

(5)   Your credit rating could use some improvement.

(6)   You hate auto repairs and dislike leaving your car at the shop.

(7)   You are an employee who uses a car for business and don't have the money to purchase the car with cash.

(8)   You quickly tire of the same car.

Results of Financial Analysis

It is better to buy when:

(1)   You pay all cash or get great finance terms such as 0% interest, or

(2)   You keep the car for 4 years or more, or

(3)   You put on more than 15,000 miles per year, or

(4)   You have impaired credit.

Depreciation methods available: There are two basic depreciation methods for business automobile, straight line and accelerated. Today's tax law further complicates matters by placing luxury car limits on depreciation. The accelerated rate (MACRS), straight line rate, and luxury limits for passenger cars for 2015 are:[17]

Year	MACRS	Straight Line	Luxury Auto	Luxury Light Truck/Van
1	20%	10%	$3,160	$3,460
2	31%	20%	$5,100	$5,600
3	19.2%	20%	$3,050	$3,350
4	11.52%	20%	$1,875	$1,975
5	11.52%	20%	$1,875	$1,975
6	5.67%	10%	$1,875	$1,975

Calculation examples: You purchase a new $40,000 car and use it 75% for business. The personal use reduces your deductions.[18] Depreciation deduction possibilities and the luxury limit are:

- $6,000 under MACRS ($40,000 x 20% x 75%)
- $3,000 under Straight Line ($40,000 x 10% x 75%)
- $2,370 under the Luxury Limit ($3,160 x 75%)

$25,000 expense election: This applies to used qualifying SUVs with a gross vehicle weight of over 6,000 pounds and used qualifying trucks with a gross vehicle weight of over 6,000 pounds and has a cargo bed under 6 feet long.

Warning: If you use your car less than 50% for business, then you can't take the 179 Expense Election.

All other passenger cars: These are subject to the luxury limits on depreciation noted on page 85. There are no tax credits and they do not qualify for the 50% bonus depreciation."

SUV Exceptions: Congress allows some exceptions where you can deduct the cost of the vehicle in the year you purchased it. These exceptions are as follows:

- The vehicle is designed for more than 9 passengers seated rearward of the driver seat.

- The vehicle is equipped with an open cargo area, or covered box, not readily accessible from the passenger compartment, of at least six feet in interior length.

- The vehicle has an integral enclosure, fully enclosing the driver compartment and load carrying device and does not have any seating that is rearward of the driver seat and has no body section protruding more than 30 inches ahead of the leading edge of the windshield. This may sound strange, but many delivery vans meet this rule.

...ng Of the Automobile *COST MINUS DEPRECIATION*

...owchart

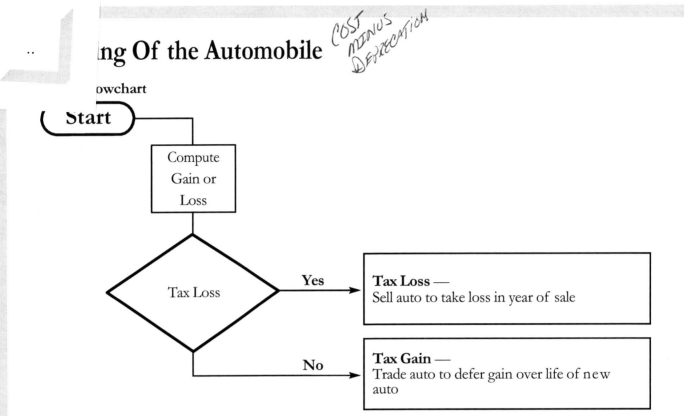

Calculation: Basis = Cost - Depreciation

Computing Gain or Loss on Disposition of Auto

Step 1: Determine Percentages of Business and Personal Use

	Business Miles	**Personal Miles**	**Total Miles**
Year 1	16,000	4,000	20,000
Year 2	13,000	2,000	15,000
Year 3	21,000	4,000	25,000
	50,000	10,000	60,000
	83.3%	16.7%	100%

Step 2: Determine Basis

	83.3% Business	**16.7% Personal**
Original cost (or basis)	$8,330	$1,670
Depreciation to date of sale	(5,248)	N/A
Basis	$3,082	$1,670

Step 3: Compute Gain or Loss

	83.3% Business	**16.7% Personal**
Selling price	$5,831	$1,169
Basis	(3,082)	(1,670)
Gain (loss)	$2,749	($ 501)

Strategy 5: Buy cars, don't lease them, to obtain the best after-tax return on your car investment.

Economics: The after-tax cost is greater to lease than to purchase both business and personal cars. We have run the numbers in detail and found that it costs about 10% more to lease than to purchase.

Lease inclusion for luxury cars: If the fair market value of the leased business car is greater than $15,200, you must add to your taxable income an inclusion amount from an IRS table found in Publication 463. The inclusion amount is designed to produce a lease payment benefit equal to the benefit you would otherwise receive from a deduction for depreciation.[20]

Strategy 6: Identify supplies and equipment used to maintain your business car.

Overview: Take a trip through your garage and basement, or wherever you store tools and cleaning supplies. Make a list of the items you use on your car. You will probably find a battery charger, battery cables, and maybe even a battery tester. You might find a tire pump, a vise, a buffer, and a sander. By the time you get to the small tools such as screwdrivers, pliers, and wrenches, you should have found a number of items whose cost you have overlooked.

Depreciate items with cost in excess of $100. If an item has an original cost in excess of $100, it should be capitalized and depreciated. If the cost is less than $100 for an individual item or a group of small tools, it's normal to expense such items in the year of purchase.

Proof: Since you will be backtracking through past acquisitions, it's likely you won't have receipts. Take photographs which can represent reasonable substitute evidence.

The reconstruction method requires a reasonable basis for the reconstruction: As I note in my workbook, you may reconstruct records that you don't have (with some exceptions such as having receipts for charitable contributions of $250 or more). The key is that there must be a reasonable basis for the reconstruction. You can't use what I call the "finger in the wind" technique.

Strategies to Get The Maximum Dollar Benefits When You Rid Yourself Of Your Current Business Car

Strategy 7: Sell cars that produce deductible losses, but trade cars that produce taxable profits.

Flowchart: See the flowchart at the left for a graphic description of what should be done.

Compute gain or loss: Follow the three simple steps at the bottom of the flowchart to determine gain or loss. Note how computations are made for both personal and business use.

Computing basis after a trade: When you trade your old car for a replacement, you take the old depreciated basis and add cash boot to determine the new basis for depreciation.[21]

Example: You give the dealer $10,000 plus your old 80% business use car to obtain the replacement car. Your basis in the old car is $2,000 for business and $2,400 for personal. For depreciation purposes, your business basis in the replacement car is $8,000 cash boot plus $2,000 from the old business basis for a total of $10,000.

Notes

Strategy 8: Sell cars on which you claimed IRS mileage rate deductions because such car **have a high basis.** Do you use IRS rates and trade cars? If so, you could be looking at a tax windf year. The low depreciation with IRS rates produces a high basis which you continue to build when trade cars.

Personal losses are not deductible: If you sell a personal car at a loss, the loss is not deductible.[23]

Personal profits are taxable: If you sell a personal car at a gain, the gain is taxable.[24]

Strategies To Audit Proof Your Business Automobile Tax Deductions

Strategy 9: Apply the new rules to increase your deductible business miles.

Business use rules: IRS requires you to separate business from personal use.[25] Your business use percentage determines your business automobile deductions.[26] If your corporation provides a car to you or to other employees, or if you are self-employed and you provide a car to your employees, the personal use percentage determines additional employee compensation.[27]

Home is principal place of business: If your home is your principal place of business, as defined in Chapter 6, all business stops from your home are business mileage with the exception of a direct commute to the office for your main job.[28] Thus, home based business owners, and some others who use their home as a principal office become winners here.

Residence is not the principal place of business: If you are traveling outside your normal geographic area where you normally conduct business, then all round-trip mileage to these business stops constitutes business mileage.[28, 30]

Example: Samantha lives in Grand Rapids, but has a business meeting in Detroit. She may deduct all her mileage to Detroit since this is outside the normal geographic area where she conducts business.

Travel within geographic area: If your home is not your principal place of business, your first stop and all business stops thereafter would be business mileage if:

- You went to the first stop for business reasons, AND
- Your first stop was a temporary business stop

A temporary business stop is one that you don't make regularly and that you will not be visiting for more than one year.[29] Since you are expected to go to the same bank and post office for more than a year, going to these places from your home would not be a temporary business stop and would be considered nondeductible mileage.

Example: John goes from his home to meet a prospect for business. He then goes to business stops A, B, C, and then to his office. All other stops would be deemed business mileage.

# of Business Mileage

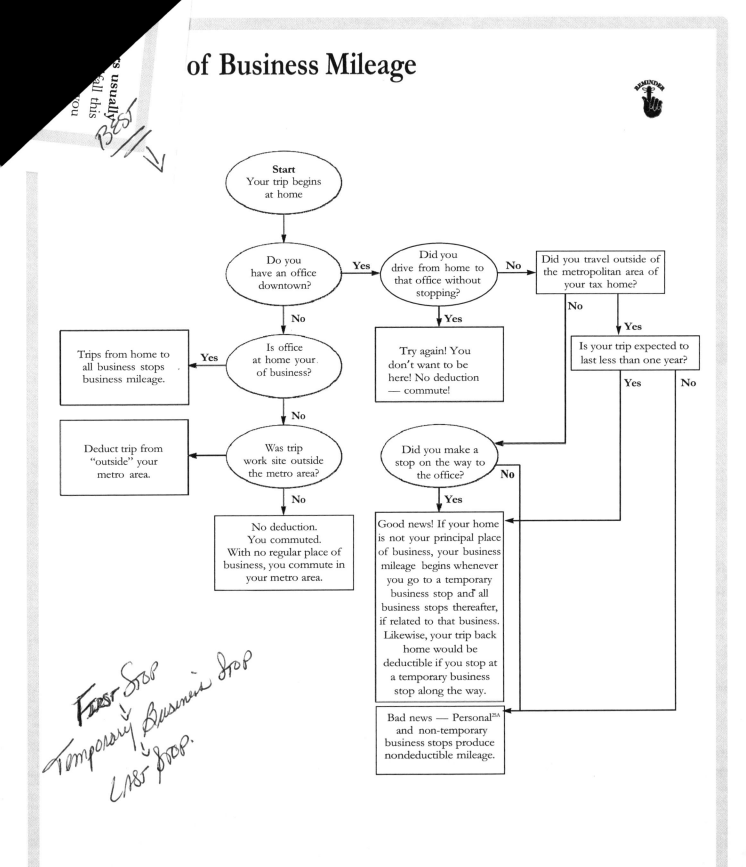

Start
Your trip begins at home

Do you have an office downtown? — **Yes** → Did you drive from home to that office without stopping? — **No** → Did you travel outside of the metropolitan area of your tax home?

No ↓ (from "Do you have an office downtown?")

Is office at home your . of business? — **Yes** → Trips from home to all business stops business mileage.

Did you drive from home to that office without stopping? — **Yes** ↓ → Try again! You don't want to be here! No deduction — commute!

Did you travel outside of the metropolitan area of your tax home? — **No** ↓ / **Yes** → Is your trip expected to last less than one year? — **Yes** / **No**

No ↓ (from "Is office at home your . of business?")

Was trip work site outside the metro area? — **Yes** → Deduct trip from "outside" your metro area.

Did you make a stop on the way to the office? — **No**

Was trip work site outside the metro area? — **No** ↓ → No deduction. You commuted. With no regular place of business, you commute in your metro area.

Did you make a stop on the way to the office? — **Yes** ↓

Good news! If your home is not your principal place of business, your business mileage begins whenever you go to a temporary business stop and all business stops thereafter, if related to that business. Likewise, your trip back home would be deductible if you stop at a temporary business stop along the way.

Bad news — Personal[25A] and non-temporary business stops produce nondeductible mileage.

First Stop
Temporary Business Stop
Last Stop.

Note: if you have NO tax home or office that you regularly go to (such as you are constantly an itinerant worker), your first business stop is not deductible and your last business stop to your home isn't deductible. All business stops in between are deductible (see IRS Publication 535).

OR: John stops at the bank first and then goes to meet a prospect for business. Mileage to the bank would not be deductible but the trip to the client would be.

Example: Jan, a real estate professional, represents a developer. She is expected to be at the model home selling homes until all homes and sites are sold, which is expected to be within one year or less. She receives a letter to this effect. She may deduct all round-trip mileage to the site.

Note: In the above example, if Jan did not sell all the home sites within one year, all mileage incurred after the one year period ends and would be deemed commuting.

Warning: Stops at the bank or post office on a weekly or daily basis are **not** deemed temporary stops. You must perform business services such as meeting clients or prospects, picking up "for sale" signs, or delivery of policies, etc.

Flowchart: The flowchart at the left gives you an easy-to-follow guide for determining business miles. Note that each trip taken through the flowchart starts at home.

Strategy 10: Keep a daily log of car use for 90 days.

The perjury set up: When you file your tax return, you or your corporation will have to answer specific questions regarding business automobiles.[31] The questions are part of your tax return and you answer the questions under penalty of perjury.[32]

The dreaded questions: The first question you will have to answer is: Do you have evidence to support business use?[33] The next question: Is the evidence written?[34] To sustain your business automobile deductions, you must be in a position to answer "yes" to both questions.

Questions: IRS Forms 4562 and 2106 also ask other questions regarding the miles driven during the year. In your tax return, you must report miles driven during the year broken down by:[35]

- Total miles
- Total commuting miles
- Total business miles
- Other personal miles (non-commuting)

Records must be adequate: Adequate records or other sufficient evidence must be kept to support business use.[36] An adequate record[37] is one made at or near the time of business use.[38] Other sufficient evidence is acceptable only if you have direct corroborative evidence (such as statements from witnesses) or other documentary evidence.[39] With automobiles, you do not need receipts for gas, parking, or tolls that are each under $75.00.[40]

Adequate records required even with IRS mileage rates: You need an adequate record of your business mileage even if you deduct your automobile expenses using IRS mileage rates.[41] The mileage rate eliminates the need to keep gas and oil receipts,[42] but it does not eliminate the need for mileage records to be broken down into business, personal, and commuting categories.[43]

Clarification: Mileage from one business stop to another business stop is business mileage. If you go to a temporary business stop for your business, but then go to an unrelated business stop, such as your regular job, you may only deduct your mileage to temp business stop, and <u>not</u> to the unrelated business stop.

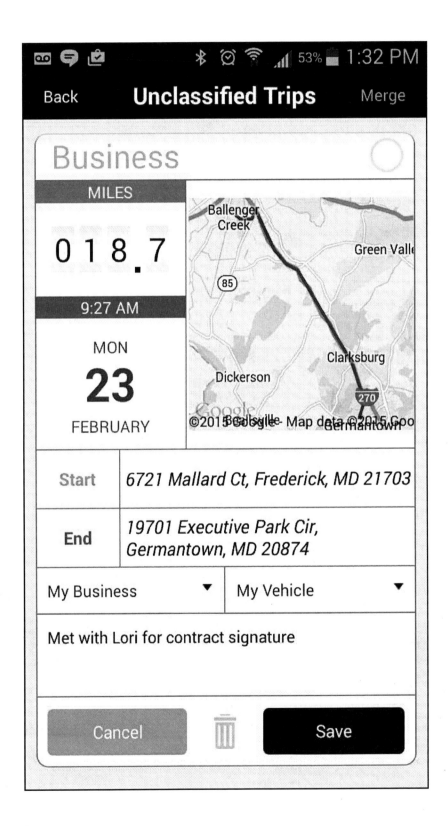

Visit our web site at: www.taxreductioninstitute.com

Penalties: Failure to keep good records exposes you to huge penalties. Moreover, Congress wants IRS to start asking for fraud penalties when taxpayers don't have good records of automobile business use.[44]

Perfect one day log: The perfect one day record is shown on the page on the left. You list all appointments both business and personal in the diary. When you use the car to get to an appointment you list the mileage next to the appointment. At the end of the day, you record your final odometer reading. Finally, you tally your business, personal, and commuting mileage and reconcile those numbers with your beginning and ending odometer.

Simplifying Methods

The 90 day log rule: IRS regulations allow a mileage record for a representative portion of the year to substantiate business use for the entire year.[45] In the first example IRS says you can keep detailed mileage records for the first three months of the year to substantiate the entire year if your business use of the vehicle follows the same pattern for the remaining nine months of the year.[46]

First week rule: The second IRS example assumes that you keep an automobile log for the first week of each month and then can prove by adequate records that your business use for the remainder of each month was consistent with that of the first week.[47]

Appointments are key: The key element to a sample record is to enter all appointments in your appointment book This proves consistent business use.

No hassle method: If you list your daily appointments in your diary, your ninety-day test can be made by:

1. Documenting beginning and ending ninety-day and annual mileage

2. Recording personal miles each day during the ninety-day test[48]

3. Recording commuting miles each day during the ninety-day test

4. Applying percentages from the test to annual mileage

Remember, this method works only if appointments are recorded and substantiate the business mileage. In addition, you must keep track of your appointments to show that the time period chosen truly represents the business activities for the entire year.[49]

Caution: Despite allowing this statistical approach in IRS regulations, some examiners have disallowed it under the presumption that it does not substantiate the rest of the year.

Note: You can not use the "simplifying method" if you use a second car during the year.[50]

Notes

Daily Appt & Mileage

DEB — Stage By 3

The Perfect Expense Log

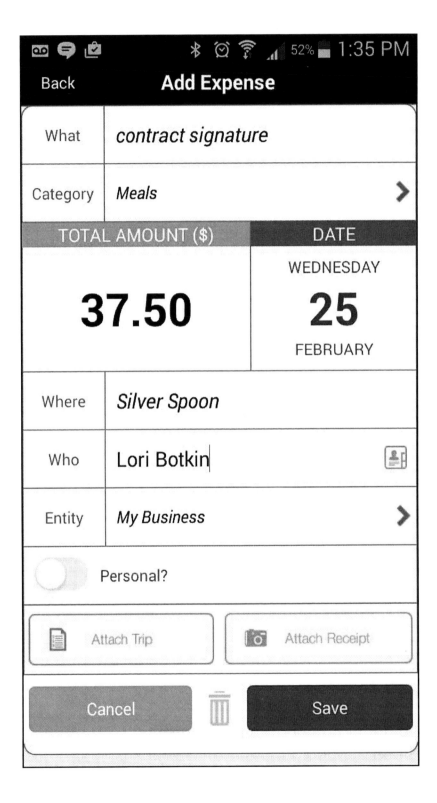

Automobile Summary

Strategies to increase daily deductions

1. Use two cars for business

2. Convert personal cars to business use

3. Pick greater of actual expenses or IRS mileage rate deductions

4. Select fastest depreciation method

5. Buy rather than lease cars

6. Identify and deduct supplies and equipment used with your business car

Strategies to get maximum dollar benefits when you rid yourself of your current business car

7. Sell cars that produce deductible losses, but trade cars that produce taxable profits

8. Sell cars on which you claimed IRS rates

Strategies to audit proof your business automobile tax deductions

9. Apply the new business mile definitions to increase your deductible mileage

10. Keep a 90-day daily log of car use

5. Get Your Maximum Business Automobile Deductions

1. Treas. Reg. §§ 1.162-1(a) and 1.162-2. <u>Commissioner v. Griner</u>, 71-2 U.S.T.C. ¶9714 (N.D. Fla.) and <u>Commissioner v. Cavender</u>, 71-2 U.S.T.C. ¶ 9723 (S.D. W.Va.).

2. Temp. Treas. Reg. 1.274-6T, 1.274-5T(b), 1.274-5T(c) of the IRC. See also IRS Pub. 17 (2001).

3. See note 1, above.

4. IRC § 1001, 1012, 1016.

5. Treas. Reg. § 1.167(g)-1. Technically, the basis for depreciation is the lower of adjusted basis under IRC § 1011 (generally, cost) or market value at the date of conversion to business use.

6. IRC §§ 1011 and 1012.

7. Treas. Reg. § 1.167(g)-1.

8. Ibid.

9. IR Notice: 2013-80, Section 2 (2013-52 IRB821)

10. Rev. Proc. 2010-51, IRB 898.

11. Ibid.

12. Rev. Proc. 2010-51.

13. Rev. Proc. 2010-51, I.R.B.

14. Rev. Proc. 95-54 & Rev. Proc. 2010-51 See Footnote 9, IBID

15. IBID and IRS Publication 463.

16. IBID and IRS Publication 463.

17. IRC § 280F(a)(2)(A); Rev. Proc. 2015-19

18. § 1.263(a) 1(b) of the Regs. <u>Cincinnati, New Orleans & Texas Pacific Railway Companies vs. Commissioner</u>; 424 F.2d 563 (Ct. CL. 1997); and of the Regs. <u>Metro Corp vs. Commissioner</u>; 116 TC 211 (2001).

18. American Taxpayer Relief Legislation of 2012

19. § 280F(a)(1)(c) of the IRC.

20. § 1.263(a) (b) of the Regs.

21. IRC §§ 263, 167 and 168. See also IRS Pub. 917.

22. Use of a minimum capitalization policy has received specific court approval as early as <u>Cincinnati, New Orleans & Texas Pac. Ry. v. U.S.</u>, 70-1 U.S.T.C. ¶ 9344, 424 F.2d 563 (Ct. Cl. 1970). IRS recognizes the fact that precedent supports such policies but remains reluctant to endorse their use officially. See Internal Revenue Manual, Part IV § 411(2).

23. IRC § 262 and Treas. Reg. § 1.262-1(b)(4).

24. IRC § 1001.

25. Temp. Treas. Reg. § 1.274-5T(b)(6)(i)(B) and (d)(2).

26. IRC §§ 274(d)(4) and 280F(d)(4)(A)(i) and Temp. Treas. Reg. §§ 1.274-5T(d)(2) and 1.280F-6T(d).
<u>David Burelson</u>, T.C. Memo 1994-130.

27. Technically speaking, personal use determines the amount of the fringe benefit reportable by your corporation and included in your income, if either the "vehicle cents per mile" or "commuting valuation" methods of valuing the fringe benefit is used. If the "annual lease value" method is used and if your corporation does not treat the automobile use as a "working condition fringe benefit" excluded from your gross income under § IRC 132, the entire annual lease value is included in your gross income; and you then deduct the portion attributable to business use. If the "annual lease value" method is used and the car is treated as a "working condition fringe benefit", only the personal-use portion of the annual lease value is included in your gross income. IRC §§ 61 and 132 and Temp. Treas. Reg. §§ 1.61-2T(d)-(f) and 1.280F- 4T(e)(1)(ii). See IRS Publications 535, "Business Expenses" (Rev. Dec. 1986) and 917, "Business Use of a Car" (Rev. Nov. 1986).

28. Rev. Rule 90-23, I.R.B. 1990-11. Modified and superseded by Rev. Rule 99-7, 1999-5 I.R.B. *Curphey vs. Comm*, 73 TC 766 (1980).

29. Rev. Rule 99-7, 1999-5 I.R.B. See also PLR 199948019 (12/7/99) and IRS Pub. 463.

30. Rev. Rule 90-23, I.R.B. 1990-11 as superseded by Rev. Rule 99-7, 1999-5 I.R.B.

31. IRS Form 2106, Depreciation and Amortization. See also Section 1.274-5T(d)(2)(1) of the IRC.

32. See declaration immediately above the signature line on IRS Forms 1040, U.S. Individual Income Tax Return, and 1120, U.S. Corporation Income Tax Return.

33. IRS Form 4562, Depreciation and Amortization.

34. Ibid.

35. Ibid.

36. IRC § 274(d).

37. IRC § 274(d) and Temp. Treas. Reg. 1.274-5T(a).

38. Temp. Treas. Reg. § 1.274-5T(c)(1) and (2)(ii)(A).

39. Temp. Treas. Reg. § 1.274-5T(c)(3).

40. 1.274-5 T(c) of the Regulations.

41. Rev. Rul. 2001-54, 2001-48 IRB 530. See also IRS Pub. 463.

42. Ibid.

43. Ibid.

44. Conference Committee Report on P.L. 99-44, as found in [1988] 8A Stand. Fed. Tax Rpt. (CCH) ¶ 5528.034.

45. Temp. Treas. Reg. § 1.274-5T(c)(3)(ii).

46. Temp. Treas. Reg. § 1.274-5T(c)(3)(ii)(C), Example (1).

47. Temp. Treas. Reg. § 1.274-5T(c)(3)(ii)(C), Example (2). See also IRS Pub. 463.

48. J.E. Frankel v. Commissioner, 27 T.C.M. 817 (1968) and B.W. Moretz, 36 T.C.M. 1341 (1977).

49. Temp. Reg. § 1.274-5T(c)(3)(ii)(C)

50. Temp. Reg. § 1.274-5T(c)(3)(ii)(B)

Notes

Notes

BUSINESS → Internet Breakout.

○ Computer dep. - 5 yrs
○ Furniture - dep. 7 yrs

○ Equipment New to You!

6 Increase Your Bottom Line When You Work At Home

Strategy 1: Depreciate assets to the extent used in business when you fail to qualify for the home office deduction.

Example: You work in an office at your home, but do not qualify for the home office deduction because the office is not used exclusively for business. Your work adds up to 80% of the use.

Result: You may depreciate the assets used 80% for business.[1]

Convert to Business Use: If you purchased the desk, file cabinet, and chair three years ago, you must convert the assets to business use under the lower of cost or market rule.[2]

Example: You have a desk you purchased three years ago. It cost you $500. It has a fair market value of $550. You depreciate 80% of the $500 because it is lower than $550.

Records: Keep records (like auto use records) of both business and personal use for 90 days.[3]

Strategy 2: Expense purchased home office assets to speed up deductions.

Special Expense Rule: Congress allows you to deduct immediately, rather than depreciate, up to $25,000 worth of business assets that you purchase during 2015.[4] The key word is "purchase." The assets may be new or used. This is allowed if your total asset purchases are less than $200,000 in 2015.

Note: As of this printing, there is a bill in Congress to raise the election to allow up to a $500,000 deduction.

Visit our web site at: www.taxreductioninstitute.com

Notes

Limitation: In order to expense the asset, the asset must be used at lease 50% for business. In addition, you cannot use the tax expense election if it will create a loss.

Example: You buy a new $1,200 rug and spend $3,000 on a used photocopier. Rather than depreciate the assets over 5 years or more, you may expense the entire $4,200 this year.

Qualifying assets: Any asset that would have qualified for the old investment tax credit is eligible for the special asset expensing break. All home office depreciable equipment meets this test.

Recapture: If you expense an asset and then your business use drops to 50% or less, you must recalculate the original expense amount as if straight line depreciation was claimed and report the difference as taxable income.[5]

Expensive Purchases: If the newly purchased assets costs $125,000, you can expense the first $25,000 and depreciate the rest.

Hot Tip: If you are going to buy more than the $25,000 expense limit, but less than $200,000, consider buying $25,000 worth of equipment in 2015 and the rest in 2016. This way you can deduct $25,000 in 2015 and the rest of your equipment in 2016 instead of depreciating the difference over 5-7 years.

Strategy 3: Qualify for the home office deduction. The home office deduction could put from $10,000 to $30,000 after tax dollars in your pocket during the next five years. See the calculation of Snyder's savings on next page.

The Home Office Rules

The Law: The Internal Revenue Code states that a home office deduction is available on to the extent that portion of the dwelling unit is used exclusively and on a regular basis as:[7]

- The principal place of business for any trade or business of the taxpayer

- A place of business that is used by patients, clients or customers in meeting or dealing with the taxpayer in the normal course of his/her trade or business, or

- In the case of a separate structure which is not attached to the dwelling unit, in connection with the taxpayer's trade or business.

Notes

How Snyder Benefits From the Home Office Deduction

Facts: Snyder files a joint tax return with his wife. The Snyders earn $150,000 in taxable income. That puts them in the 31% federal and 10% state income tax bracket. Mrs. Snyder earns $78,000 from her job as an employee in town. Mr. Snyder works out of his home and earns net taxable income of $72,000, which is reported in Schedule C of their Form 1040.

First Year Tax Refund

	Total	Home Office Percentage	Home Office Deduction	Tax Benefit Rate	Tax Refund
Mortgage interest	$10,401	15.84%	$1,648	13.02%	$215
Real estate taxes	947	15.84%	150	13.02%[1]	20
Utilities	1,704	15.84%	270	54.02%[2]	146
Homeowner's insurance	310	15.84%	49	54.02%	26
General repairs	600	15.84%	95	54.02%	51
Pest control	400	15.84%	63	54.02%	34
Repairs to office	200	100%	200	54.02%	108
Depreciation-furniture	1,886	100%	1,886	54.02%	1,019
Depreciation-home	2,545	15.84%	403	54.02%	218
Snyder's cash-in-pocket from home office deduction					$1,837

Economic Results

Cash from home office deduction	$1,837
Cash from extra business mileage	582[3]
Total first year cash	2,419
6% annuity due factor for 5 years	x 5.9753
Net cash after 5 years	$14,454

[1]Self-Employment tax rate

[2]13.02 self-employment tax rate plus 31% federal tax rate plus 10% state tax rate

[3]Snyder's home business allows him to reduce his personal mileage and increase his business auto expense by $1,077. Thus, $582 is refunded by the tax collectors ($1,077 x 54.02%).

In addition, in the case of an employee, the home office deduction is allowed only if the exclusive use is for the convenience of the employer.[8]

Method one is to do your most important tasks at home: The Supreme Court decision in Soliman[9] interpreted what constitutes a "principal place of business" for purposes of the home office deduction. The courts defined the "principal place" as where you perform your most important tasks of the business such as where you make the cash register ring or where you see clients or patients.

Method two is the time test: If there is no one spot from which you perform your most important tasks or is hard to tell where you perform your most important tasks, the Court adopted a "time test," which asks whether you performed over one-half your working hours in your home office.

Soliman's Office: Dr. Soliman was an anesthesiologist who performed services at three hospitals for 30 to 35 hours per week. He was provided with no office space at the hospitals. He used a home office 10-15 hours per week to:

    🌐 Have telephone conversations with patients and other medical doctors.

    🌐 Conduct his research and design treatments for his new and existing patients.

    🌐 Write up and maintain patient logs and medical records

    🌐 Study for any continuing education in his home office.

Dr. Soliman had no other office in which these were performed.

Dreadful Decision: The court ruled that Soliman gets no deduction for an office in his home despite the following facts:

- Soliman's home was integral and essential to his business.

- The office was used exclusively for business on a regular basis.

The Soliman Quiz: You should either regularly see clients or customers and close sales in your home office OR spend more than one-half your total work time working in your home office.

If you answered "no" to the above questions, your home office deduction could be lost under the Supreme Court decision. As you can see, this was a bad decision for most businesses.

Method 3 is to use the Congressional exception to Soliman: Starting in 1999, Congress liberalized the home office rules making it much easier for many people to claim a home office deduction. They did this by carving an exception to Soliman. Now your home office qualifies as a "principal place of business" for the home office deduction if:

1. The office is used to conduct <u>administrative</u> or <u>management</u> activities for a trade or business, and

2. There is no other office where you conduct substantial administrative or management activities.[10]

Thus, if you do your logs, contact patients, or customers, listen to educational tapes, read business related materials and prepare bills for customers than you're rendering administrative activities.

 Visit our web site at: www.taxreductioninstitute.com

Notes

Insignificant Services Elsewhere: The fact that you do some administrative services elsewhere won't count against you if these services are not substantial. Thus, if you occasionally do some paperwork elsewhere, this won't disqualify you from the home office deduction. Keeping a good log of where you work is vital if you have more than one office.[11] In fact, even if an office is provided you, you can still opt to work out of your home and perform all of your administrative activities out of your home.[12]

Example: John, a self-employed plumber, spends most of his time in homes repairing and installing plumbing. He has an office at home that he uses exclusively and regularly for his administrative and management activities such as billing customers, making appointments, and ordering supplies. His home qualifies as a principal office for the home office deduction.[13]

Example: Margie is a realtor. She is provided an office by her broker but opts to perform almost all of her administrative activities out of her home. She does all cold calling and mailings from her home. She does her logs at home. She reads her continuing education at home and compares comparable price sheets from her home computer. She only goes into the office when she has phone duty, sales meetings, to turn in contracts, and to meet clients. Margie's home would qualify as a "principal place of business" for the home office deduction.

Consider the home office safe harbor approach: Starting in 2013, IRS has allowed a simplified "safe harbor" approach for the home office. A home office deduction can be an important tax break for small and home based businesses. However, the deduction requires calculations of depreciation and allocation of various home owner expenses based on the part of the home that qualifies for a home office. IRS felt that this might have involved more work than the deduction was worth. Accordingly, they adopted a simplified approach.

This simplified approach is in alternative to the calculation of depreciation and allocation of expenses to the home office. Starting in 2013, home business owners have the option of using the regular approach for the home office or of multiplying the square footage used for business by $5, for a maximum deduction of $1,500.

However, unlike the name "safe harbor approach," you are required to meet all of the home office rules that allow for the deduction. Thus, if you are self-employed you must use an exclusive portion of your home regularly as either your:

- Principal place of business or
- Where you meet patients, clients or customers or
- As a separate structure on your property used exclusively for business or
- As a place to store inventory

Employees must also meet a rule that the home office is set up for the convenience of the employer.

Note: Frankly, I don't see the safe harbor approach being very useful. It does make the tax return easier; however, it doesn't give you any depreciation, which could be a big deal, doesn't allow for any allocation of interest and taxes, which could reduce your social security and Medicare Taxes and doesn't allow for any other home office expenses. The optional safe harbor approach is in lieu of all other home office deduction. You should probably test both approaches to see which is best for you, but in most cases, the optional approach will result in about one third or less the deductions that the normal method would have provided.

Maximizing Home Office Square Footage

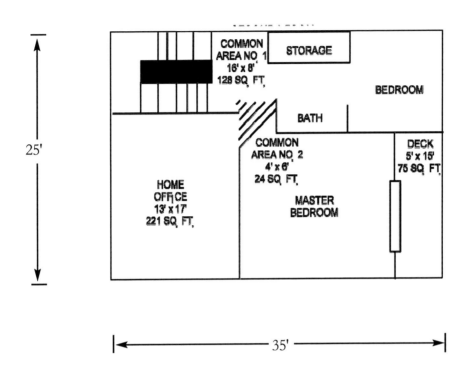

Three Choices:

1. Number of rooms office occupies, divided by total rooms in house.
2. Total square footage office occupies as a percentage of total square footage in house.
3. Net square footage applicable to office use.

Computation Of Net Square Footage:

Total square footage 25' x 35' x 2 floors		1,750
Deduct:		
Common areas:		
First floor entry and stairway	128	
Second floor stairway and landing	128	
Second floor common area	24	
Deck (not a living area)	75	355
Net square footage base		1395

Analysis Of Choices Based On:

1. Number of rooms 1/8 – 12.50%
2. Total square footage 221/1675 (1750 – 75 for deck) = 13.19%
3. Net square footage 221/1395 = 15.84%

Winners: The clear winners are those that have a home based business such as network marketers and consultants as well as free-lance writers and freelance musicians who choose to work from their home. Anyone who works at home and performs most of their administrative activities for their business from their home in an exclusive portion of their home will be a winner!

Other Home Office Requirements

1. **Exclusive use:** The term "exclusive use" means just that.[14] No personal or other non-qualifying work activities may occur in your home office area.[15]

   Part of a Room: A portion of a room can qualify as a home office, but all business items must be located in the same contiguous area and there should be some physical separation of the business area from the personal area.[16] A movable partition (also deductible) can be used to define the home office area.

2. **Regular use:** IRS code does not define regular use. However, the courts indicate that using your home office 3 to 4 times for a total of 10 to 12 hours a week should be regular.[17]

   Principal Place of Business: There are three ways in which your home qualifies as a principal place of business.

Strategy 4: Use the meet and greet test to qualify for the home office deduction.

Exception to general rule: If you do not use your home office as your principal place of business, another way to qualify for the deduction is to use the home office as a place to meet or deal with clients, patients, and prospects in the normal course of your business.[18] This exception applies only if the use of the home office by your clientele is substantial and integral to conducting your business.[19] Occasional meetings are insufficient to make this exception applicable.[20]

Physical presence required: The key words for this exception are "meet or deal" with clients, patients, or customers. This demands a physical presence of patients or customers, not just a telephone presence, no matter how extensive or frequent the telephone conversations.[21]

Regular: The meeting and dealing must be on a regular basis.[22] How often is regular? How often must you meet with clients, customers, patients, or prospects for such meetings to constitute normal course of business? At a minimum, you must prove that such meetings are ordinary, usual occurrences in your business - not occasional, spur-of-the-moment, or last-minute accommodations to someone's schedule.[23] In other words, home office meetings must be integral to the way you conduct your business.

Strategy 5: Qualify for the home office deduction by using a separate structure in connection with your business.

You may qualify for a home office deduction if, in connection with your trade or business, you use a separate structure not attached to your dwelling unit. [24] The separate structure must be used exclusively and on a regular basis for business.[25] It need not be your principal place of business or a place where you deal with customers, clients, or patients.[26] Examples of structures that meet the separate structure requirements are an artist's studio, a florist's greenhouse, and a carpenter's workshop.

Strategy 6: Inventory and Product Samples.

A deduction is now allowed when used on a regular basis to either store inventory and/or product samples if you are in a business of selling products at retail or wholesale and if your residence is the sole fixed location for that business.[27]

Notes

Strategies That Build Bigger Tax Benefits

Strategy 7: Avoid taxable income when you sell your home.

Universal exclusion rule overview: If you sell your home after May 6, 1997, a fabulous new universal exclusion applies to you at any age. You now can avoid up to $500,000 of profit (if married filing jointly), or $250,000 (if single).[28]

Prior Depreciation Taken: If you have taken any depreciation on your home after May 6, 1997 either from a home office deduction or by treating the home as a rental property, you must separate the gain on the sale of the old house into two parts: depreciation taken and other gains.

Example: John and Mary claimed a home office deduction for their network marketing business. If the house has appreciated to $100,000 but they got $10,000 of depreciation, John and Mary will have to pay tax on the $10,000 at their normal income tax rates.[29]

Exclusion rule: Although the normal exclusion amount is $250,000, married couples get to exclude up to $500,000 of gain if:[30]

- They file jointly, and

- Either spouse owned the house for two of the last five years, and

- Both spouses used the home as their principal residences for two out of the last five years, and

- Neither spouse has claimed the exclusion within the last two years.

The two year requirements as to ownership and use need not be the same two out of five years.[31]

If only one spouse meets these rules, you may utilize the $250,000 exclusion. This will also apply to newly married couples.

Single people will get the $250,000 exclusion if they individually meet the two year ownership and use rules and haven't used the exclusion within the past two years.

Observation: You can, therefore, use the exclusion every two years.

Exceptions for forced sales: Congress enacted some relief for you if you are required to sell your house before the two year period of occupancy expires or even if you have used the exclusion less than two years ago.

If you have a change in employment, health or other unforeseen circumstances (e.g. divorce, multiple births, job changes / job losses), then you may be entitled to a partial exclusion.[31]

Guest Book For Home Office

Work Activity Log for Typical Morning

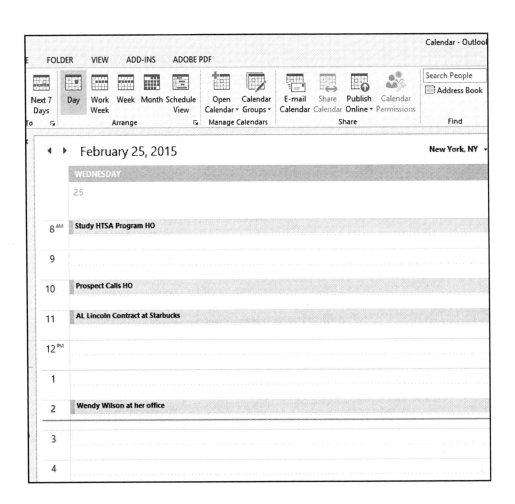

Visit our web site at: www.taxreductioninstitute.com

Example: Lori sells her house because she has a new job in another town. On the date of sale, she has owned her principal residence for 18 months. She has never excluded gain from another home sale. If she had lived there for two years, she would avoid up to $250,000 of gain. However, since she didn't meet the two year occupancy requirement because of a job change, she can exclude 18/24 of the $250,000 or $187,500.

Note: By not meeting the rules due to unforeseen circumstances, you still get a partial exclusion.

Strategies To Bullet-Proof And Retain Home Office Deductions

Strategy 8: Photograph the office.

You use a home office today, but will you use it tomorrow? There's no way to know for certain, so take a photograph of your office to prove that it actually existed. To prove when the office existed, establish the vintage of your photograph with a processing date. Most photofinishers print the processing date on the back of the photograph. Make sure your photograph is processed by such an establishment.

Strategy 9: Prove your home office space.

Keep blueprints of your home to prove the amount of space occupied by the home office. If blueprints are not available, make a drawing of your home showing the relationship of the home office's square footage to the total square footage of the home.

Strategy 10: Prominently display your home office phone number and address on business cards, stationary, and advertising.

You must be able to prove that you actually operated a business from your home. If economically feasible, install a separate business phone in your home. The business phone should be listed in the business's name in both the white and yellow pages. You should have business stationery with your home address on it. If you have two business addresses, they should have equal prominence on the stationery. Use your home address on your business cards. If two addresses appear, they should have equal prominence. Similarly, both phone numbers should have equal prominence.[32]

Strategy 11: Have your guests sign a guest log book when they visit your home office.

If you claim a home office deduction because you use the office in the normal course of business to meet and deal with clients, patients, and prospects, have your business visitors sign a guest book each time they come to your office. The guest book need not be formal, just a record that business contacts actually meet with you in your home office. Remember, the burden of proof is on you. If you claim use of your home office to see clients and customers, don't forget you must be able to prove that clients, patients, prospects, or colleagues were physically present in your home office.[33]

Strategy 12: Keep a time and work activity log.

A work activity log (really a meticulously annotated daily diary) offers an excellent supporting document to establish where you spend your work time. The work activity log does not need to be an elaborate document. You already have a daily diary. Simply use it as an activity log. If you are working at your home office, you could simply write "home office" (or some abbreviation) and note the time spent in the home office. Details indicating the specific type of work you are doing at home help immensely.

Notes

Strategy 13: Retain Receipts and Paid Invoices.

General rule: Canceled checks only prove that you paid the bill. You must support the canceled checks with receipts and invoices.

Expense types: When calculating your home office deduction you must consider two types of home expenses: (1) those that benefit the entire home and (2) those incurred solely as a result of the home office. You must keep receipts for both.

Entire home: You are allowed to deduct a portion of the expenses that benefit the entire home including utilities, general home maintenance, and homeowner's insurance.[34] At the end of the year, you allocate these expenses based on the business use percentage of your home.[35]

Office only: You are allowed to deduct all expenses that benefit only the home office.[36] Expenses benefiting only the home office include repairs to the home office area plus office supplies and other items purchased specifically for the home office area. There's nothing tricky about these expenses, but you must have receipts to support your expenditures.

Strategy 14: Deduct long-distance telephone charges.

Beginning in 1989, tax law allows no deduction for the first telephone into your personal residence, regardless of use.[37] Local charges are deductible only if you install a second phone in your home. Long-distance charges are deductible and should be documented.

Caution: Your home office deduction is limited to the net income from the business attributable to your home office.[38] Thus, if your net income equals $2,000 after deductions, your home office deduction would be limited to the $2,000. However, any excess can be carried forward forever.

Notes

Work At Home Summary

How you benefit when you work at home

1. Depreciate business assets to extent of business use

2. Expense purchases of business assets

3. Qualify for the home office deduction

Strategies to qualify for the home office deduction

4. Meet and greet in normal business

5. Separate structure in connection with business

6. Store inventory and product samples

Strategy to build bigger tax benefits

7. Eliminate office in year of sale to avoid taxable income

Strategies to audit proof and retain home office deductions

8. Photograph the office

9. Prove space used for home office

10. Display home office phone number and address where appropriate

11. Have business guest register in log book

12. Keep a record of your home office time in your diary book

13. Retain receipts and paid invoices

14. Deduct business-related long-distance telephone charges

Notes

6. Increase Your Bottom Line When You Work At Home

1. E.g., IRC § 280F; Sherri A. Mulne, TC Memo 1996-320

2. Reg. 1.167(g)-1.

3. Temp. Reg. § 1.274-5t(c).

4. IRC § 179 as amended by Small Busines Jobs Act 2010.

5. IRC § 280F(d)(1).

6. Section 1.168(k) 1T(b)(3)(v) of the Income Tax Regulations.

7. IRC § 280A(c)(1).

8. IRC § 280A(c).

9. Commissioner of Internal Revenue vs. Soliman, No. 91-998, Supreme Court of the U.S. (January 1993)

10. Taxpayer Relief Act (TRA) page 932, which amends section 280(A)(c)(1) of the IRC.

11. Research Institute of America Report on Taxpayer Relief Act of 1997/ (HR 2014), Page 460.

12. H. Report 105-148 (PL 105-34), page 407.

13. IRS Publication 587

14. See Gomez V. Commissioner, 41 T.C.M. 585 (1980); Prop. Reg. § 1.280A-2(g).

15. A.W. Hamacher, 94 TC_, No. 21, CCH Dec. 46,444 (1990).

16. Gomez v. Commissioner, 41 T.C.M. 585 (1980); Prop. Reg. § 1.280A-2(g). See also Jack C.C. Huang; TC Summary Opinion 2002-93 (7/18/02).

17. See Green v. Commissioner, 78 T.C. 428 (1982)
   (2 1/4 hours a night, 5 nights a week), rev'd on another issue, 83-1 USTC q9387 (9th Cir. 1983).

18. IRC § 280A(c)(1)(B) and Prop. Treas. Reg. § 1.280A-2(c).

19. Prop. Treas. Reg. § 1.280A-2(c).

20. Ibid.

21. Green v. Commissioner, 707 F.2d 404, 83-1 U.S.T.C. 9387 (9th Cir. 1983); Frankel v. Commissioner, 82 T.C. 318 (1984); Prop. Treas. Reg. § 1.280A-2(c).

22. Frankel, supra.

23. Jackson, supra.

24. IRC § 280A(c)(1)(C) and Prop. Treas. Reg. § 1.280A-2(d).

25. Ibid.

26. IRC § 280A(c)(1)(C); Scott v. Commissioner, 84TC 683 (1985). Scott involved two issues: the first concerned the "separate structure" exception and the second concerned application of the gross income limitation. Congress nullified the Scott case on the court's interpretation of gross income. The court's decision on the separate structure is still valid.

27. § 280A(c)(1)(C).

28. Taxpayer Relief Act of 1997, § 312 also see § 121(a) of the Internal Revenue Code.

29. Taxpayer Relief Act of 1997, § 311 also see § 121(d)(6) of the Internal Revenue Code.

30. Taxpayer Relief Act of 1997, § 312 also see § 121(b)(2)B & 121(b)(2)(c) of the Internal Revenue Code.

31. IBID and Rev. Rul. 80.172, 1982 CB 56.

32. <u>Jackson vs. Comm,</u> 76TC 696 (1981); <u>Heuer vs. Comm,</u> 32TC 947 (1959).

33. Prop. Treas. Reg. § 1.280A-2(c).

34. Prop. Treas. Reg. § 1.280A-2(i)(5)(ii).

35. Prop. Treas. Reg. § 1.280A-2(i).

36. Prop. Treas. Reg. § 1.280A-2(i)(5)(ii).

37. P.L. 100-647 § 5073, enacting new IRC § 262(b).

38. Section 280A(c)(5).

Notes

Notes

7 IRS Audits

Overview

Fear: IRS wants you to be afraid. It selects returns for audit for a variety of reasons including the creation of fear.

Jail: During the heart of the tax season, IRS releases prison stories about those taxpayers who have tried to cheat on their tax returns. The release of information is timed so that while you are putting together the information for your tax return, you are reading about people who are going to prison.

IRS Personnel with Whom You Deal

Taxpayer service representatives: When you call the IRS information service to get a question answered, you talk to a taxpayer service representative. A taxpayer service representative is someone with a two-year associate degree - two years of college in any field, with no requirement for any accounting or tax courses. These are the people who answer your tax questions. The reps do get some training. Three days of classroom training are required for reps who assist persons wishing to file Form 1040A. There's also a 20-day basic training course for the people who answer the phones. After the basic training, an individual is IRS qualified to answer phone-in questions.

Chances of An IRS Audit

Income Level	Percent Audited		
	In 2011	In 2012	In 2013
Individual Return Nonbusiness			
No Earned Income Credit			
Under $200,000	0.5	0.5	0.4
Under $200K Schedule E or Form 2108	1.0	1.1	1.0
$200,000-$1,000,000	3.2	2.8	2.5
Individual Return Business (not Farm)			
No Earned Income Credit			
Under $25,000	1.3	1.2	1.0
$25,000-$100,000	2.9	2.4	2.3
$100,000-$200,000	4.3	3.6	3.0
$200,000-$1,000,000	3.8	3.4	2.7
$1,000,000 and above	12.5	12.1	10.8
Partnership Return	0.4	0.5	0.4
S Corporation Return*	0.4	0.5	0.4
Corporation Return (Based on Assets)			
Under $250,000	0.9	0.9	0.8
$250,000-$1,000,000	1.6	1.7	1.3
$1,000,000-$5,000,000	1.9	2.1	1.4
$5,000,000-$10,000,000	2.6	2.6	2.0
$10,000,000-$50,000,000	13.3	10.5	15.8
$50,000,000-$100,000,000	18.9	20.7	7.0
$100,000,000-$250,000,000	16.6	23.2	15.5
$250,000,000-$500,000,000	17.4	22.7	19.4
$500,000,000-$1,000,000,000	20.6	22.7	22.5

Pursuant to "Internal Revenue Service Data Book; Table 9. Examination Coverage."

*Note: IRS announced it will be increasing audits for S Corporations.

Call the IRS at your own peril: The IRS does not stand behind its answers. If it answers your question incorrectly, you're stuck and must pay the proper tax.

Take names: When IRS gives you an incorrect answer and you reasonably rely on it, you can avoid penalties if you have the name of the IRS person who gave you the bad information.

Tax auditors: Your tax return will be examined either by a tax auditor or a revenue agent. If you are going to an IRS office to present your information, you will in all likelihood be visiting a tax auditor. To qualify, a tax auditor must have a four-year college degree - in anything. Tax auditors generally start at half of what the big accounting firms pay.

No thinking allowed: The office auditor is generally not required to interpret guidelines or engage in research. The issues in contention are clearly defined by a classifier before the returns are assigned to individual examiners. Any expansion beyond that must be approved by the group manager.

Revenue agents: Revenue agents must have a four-year college degree and a minimum of 24 semester hours of accounting. Experience can be substituted for the 24 hours of accounting. IRS does not recruit all "A" students. Many of the revenue agents squeak through college with "C" averages. The "A" students are snapped up by the big accounting firms.

Like the Army: Revenue agents are expected to be and usually are good soldiers. That's important. For the IRS system to work, revenue agents must believe that it is their IRS, right or wrong. They learn tax law the way IRS teaches it and wants them to see it. Revenue agents go through extensive training at IRS to learn the way IRS wants things done. They handle complex returns which require full use of their accounting skills. Unlike the tax auditor, the revenue agent sets the entire scope of the examination. Revenue agents are also underpaid in comparison to their contemporaries at the big accounting firms.

Notes

IRS Call
1. Name
2. Badge #
3. date of Call
4. Time of Call
5. what was the Question you asked them
6. What was the Answer they gave you.

Tax Auditors

Notes

Ten Ways To Reduce Your Chances Of An IRS Audit

1. Mail your return by Certified Mail Return Receipt Requested: If the IRS Regional Service Center fails to your tax return, you automatically increase your chances of being audited. To make sure you're not taking unnecessary chances, send your tax return by Certified Mail Return Receipt Requested, overnight delivery,[1] or I like "E-Filing" which prints a receipt and processes your refund quicker.

2. Send changes of address to the IRS: File Form 8822 "Change of Legal Address" whenever you move. This will ensure that you will get any refund. In addition, any notices that IRS sends you can be at the last known address. If you move, you may be liable to the IRS without knowledge since you didn't tell them of the move.

3. Make sure your tax return is neat: Your tax return does not have to be typed, but it must be neat and easy to read. Legible tax returns create an impression of attention to detail.

4. File all elections: There are certain tax breaks and options that require the filing of an election. Sometimes the filing can be done by merely picking a method of reporting. It's generally better to attach separate statements for all elections made in a tax return. This further supports attention to detail and shows an understanding of tax law.

5. Report all income: The IRS has implemented various unreported income audit programs. Make sure your tax return: first, reports all income earned by you, and second, identifies the income by source. If you receive a Form 1099 for consulting services, report the income on a supporting schedule and include the taxpayer ID number from the 1099. Since the IRS already has the information from the 1099, you will reduce your chances of audit selection by enabling IRS to match the 1099 with your tax return.

6. Have your return prepared by a competent tax preparer: The signature of a certified public accountant, tax attorney, or enrolled agent will help minimize your chances of an audit examination.

Notes

Notes

7. Break income and expenses into small segments: Income reported to the IRS on a 1099 should be separated from other income. The separation will help IRS determine that you have indeed reported all income earned. Also, break down expenses as far as possible to explain to the IRS examiners exactly what was involved in the expenses. If, for example, you had promotional expenses of $10,000 and that's all that appeared in your tax return, your chances of audit would be significant. However, should your promotion be broken down between travel, advertising, and entertainment expenses, you may reduce the chances of audit.

8. Keep records of expert advice: If you relied on the advice of your accountant or lawyer, keep records as to the nature and date of the advice. There are cases that have waived penalties for a good faith reliance on an independent expert.[2]

9. Sign your tax return: Failing to sign a tax return is one of the biggest "Red Flags" for an audit.

10. Double check your Social Security number: This is another big mistake that taxpayers make. Always double check your Social Security number on your tax return.

Fifteen Steps For The Audit

1. Get ready when preparing your tax return: The time to get ready for an IRS audit is while you are preparing your tax return. That's the only time you have all your tax information in front of you. Reference your support to the return so that you can find it later, if you should need it. Questionable items, if any, should be supported by tax memorandums or other information from your tax advisor.

2. Don't panic: An audit notice does not indicate that anything is wrong with your return. It's simply a request by the IRS to find out if your tax return was properly prepared and to determine the proper amount of tax — no more, no less. Generally, you will be notified of the audit by mail, although you could be telephoned. If you are notified by mail, you'll be asked to telephone the examiner.

3. Limit scope of audit: In an IRS office audit, the IRS tells you what is being examined and sets the scope of the audit. Try to get the examining auditor to agree to that scope before the examination begins. The reason for limiting the scope is simple: If an issue is not raised on audit, it is not often allowed as a question at the appeals level.

Copyright © 1989-2015 Sanford Botkin

Notes

4. Burden of proof is on you: Tax law requires you to prove that your deductions are valid and that you have paid the proper amount of tax. The IRS need prove nothing. When going through your records and getting ready for the audit, make sure you keep in mind that the burden of proof is on you. None of that "innocent until proven guilty" business.

5. Dress normally: Do not make a special trip to Goodwill Industries to buy clothes for your audit. Dress and act normally during the entire audit. Do not plead poverty or stupidity. Excuses don't work.

6. Be on time: IRS examiners are graded on efficiency. If you are late for your appointment and cause the auditor to be inefficient, you start the audit in an antagonistic environment. Moreover, you have given the auditor extra time to scrutinize your records before the audit begins. Frequently, office auditors will have only 15 to 20 minutes to look over your return before you arrive. If you are late, you've expanded that time and irritated the tax auditor. Best bet: Be early.

7. Bring organized information: Make sure you are prepared to answer questions and deliver documents to the auditor. If you receive notification from the IRS about the documents you need for the audit, make sure those are organized so that you cannot only answer the questions, but also deliver the supporting documents quickly. This helps the examiner complete the audit more efficiently, get a better grade from his or her superiors, and bring the whole unpleasant task to a quick conclusion.

8. Don't volunteer information: Never say, "I've always done it that way." Don't elaborate; answer only questions asked. Be concise, and if the question does not appear to be relevant, ask why it is being asked. Bring only the documents requested in the IRS's invitation letter and do not volunteer any information concerning those documents during the audit process. When asked specific questions, answer them, but do not elaborate. In addition, be careful what you say to a revenue agent. This information can be used in a criminal trial.[3]

Notes

Document and Court Value

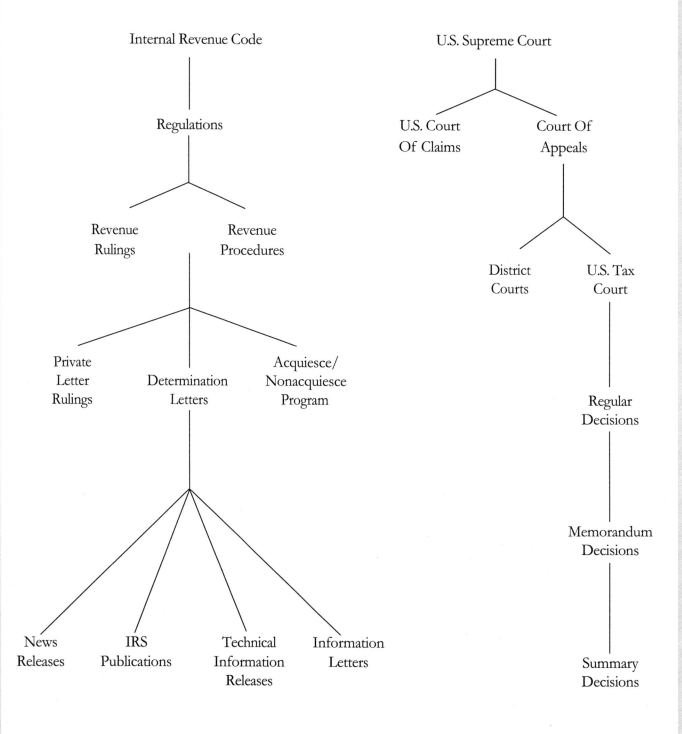

Internal Revenue Service

Internal Revenue Code

Regulations

Revenue Rulings

Revenue Procedures

Private Letter Rulings

Determination Letters

Acquiesce/ Nonacquiesce Program

News Releases

IRS Publications

Technical Information Releases

Information Letters

Courts

U.S. Supreme Court

U.S. Court Of Claims

Court Of Appeals

District Courts

U.S. Tax Court

Regular Decisions

Memorandum Decisions

Summary Decisions

9. Don't dangle ends: Do not leave or expose dangling ends for the auditor to find. If it is easy for the auditor to find something wrong, the immediate conclusion is that there must be lots of other things wrong in your return.

10. Ask for tax law references: If you think you are right, ask the auditor or agent for the legal references. Don't accept vague statements or interpretations of the law. Make your tax advisor the goat by saying: My accountant told me this deduction was proper, can you give me something that shows he's wrong?

11. Don't give in: The IRS Audit Manual states, "Hasty agreement to adjustments and undue concern about immediate closing of the case may indicate a more thorough examination is needed." If you appear to be a soft touch, the IRS will look for larger contributions from you.

12. Never be alone with a Special Agent: Special Agents are not special. Their job is to investigate criminal actions. If you ever have two agents see you, ask whether either of them is a special agent. If one is, terminate the meeting and seek out a good tax lawyer.

There is no privilege protecting your communications with your accountant.[4] Accordingly, never hire an accountant to represent you with a special agent. Hire a lawyer who in turn can hire an accountant.

13. Don't tamper with the evidence: No backdating of documents or intimidating of witnesses should ever occur. More people get indicted for these items than the original offense since it is easier to prove. To be safe, don't contact any witnesses for the government, let your lawyer do it.

14. Never ever die: IRS audits approximately 68% of all final returns.

15. Be careful of the Rat Fee: IRS pays a 10% commission for people to rat on you. If you want to make a living in reporting tax cheats, get publication 733 (cash rewards for turning in tax cheats).

7. IRS Audits

1. IRS Notice 2001-62

2. George S. Mauerman, T.C. Memo 1993-23.

3. Gene E. Erekson, T.C. Memo No. 94-4228.

4. Couch v. U.S. - 409 U.S. - 322 (1973).

A Appendix A — Choosing The Right Business Form

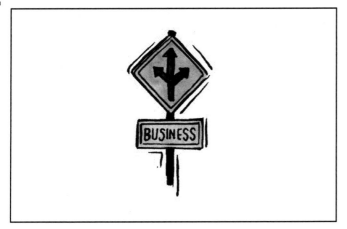

Overview: There are four basic business forms available for most business owners:

- Proprietorship (Schedule C)
- Limited Liability Company (LLC)
- Regular Corporation (C Corporation)
- S Corporation

The matrix on page 132 provides an excellent overview of the differences. This section highlights important strategies for the different forms of business.

Strategy To Keep Things Simple

Strategy 1: Use Schedule C Sole Proprietor as your form of business.

It's easiest to operate your business as a sole proprietorship. There's only one tax return to file and no corporate formalities. In fact, like an LLC, it is simple, simple, simple!

Strategy 2: Set up an LLC

The only filing with the IRS is the Schedule C with your individual tax return and, unless you have employees, there is no registration with the state, no Federal ID Number, and no Workman's Comp. The disadvantages are that the LLC requires a little more paperwork and that some states will tax an LLC higher than a sole proprietorship. Also, some foreign jurisdictions may not accept the limited liability of an LLC as they would a corporation and you can't have a self-insured medical plan set up for yourself unless you hire your spouse to perform significant services in your business.

Advantages and Disadvantages of Business Forms

Description	Schedule C Proprietorship	Regular Corporation	S Corporation
Reasonable salary	Not an issue	Deductible	Deductible
Unreasonable (excessive) salary	Not an issue	Not deductible by corporation; dividend to shareholder/employee	Generally, not an issue for shareholder/employees
Social security taxes	Self employment tax based on bottom-line Schedule C income	Taxed 50% to corporation and 50% to employee	Same as regular corporation
Net income	Taxed at individual tax rates	Taxed at corporate tax rates	Taxed at individual tax rates
Net loss	Deducted on individual return against other income; unabsorbed losses may be carried back and forward	Net loss on corporate return is carried back and forward	Deducted and carried back and forward on individual return up to shareholder's basis in stock and loans to corporation
Medical insurance premiums on owner	2015, deductible 100% on Schedule C.	Deducted on corporate return	Same as proprietorship, including ability to deduct as 100% on individual return
Disability Premiums on owner	Not deductible	Deductible to corporation; taxable to recipient of benefits	Not deductible by corporation or individual
Group term life insurance premiums on owner	Not deductible	Deductible as a tax-free fringe benefit on first $50,000 of coverage	Not deductible
Retirement benefits	Basically same as corporation	Basically same as individual	Basically same as individual
Supper money for owner	Not deductible	Deductible	Questionable
Election required	No	No	Yes — strict time limits
Ownership	Individual	Stock can be more than one class	Only individuals, estates, and trusts restricted to one class of stock (voting rights can differ)
Liquidation of ownership	Assets are sold and individual is taxed (double tax problem)	Sale of stock or sale of assets and liquidation of corporation for built-in gains	Sale of stock or assets, no double tax problem, except
Liability	Individual	Corporate, except for professional corporations wherein professionals remain liable under malpractice statutes	Same as regular corporation
Asset expensing	Up to $500,000 if assets placed in service total less than $2 million in 2014.	Claimed on corporate return with same limits that apply to an individual	Reflected on S Corporation return and claimed on individual return
Paperwork	Simplest form	Two separate entities for income tax purposes... payroll taxes...corporate minutes	Same as regular corporation; however, may involve more complex state filing requirements
Hiring child under age 18	No social security tax if child	Social Security taxes apply	Social security taxes apply (may gift stock to children and eliminate social security on distribution, in addition, can still benefit from shifting income).

Note: Sole owner LLCs who don't elect to be taxed as corporations file as sole proprietorships on schedule C. If not sole owner LLC, then it is filed as a partnership on IRS form 1065 (unless they elect to be taxed as a corporation).

Strategies To Reduce Taxes

Strategy 3: Use the S Corporation to cut your self-employment tax.

No self-employment tax: A shareholder's share of the corporation's taxable income is not self-employment income, even though it is included in gross income of the shareholder.[1]

Reasonable compensation: Services performed by shareholder/owners must be reasonably compensated. Reasonable compensation is subject to wide discretion. It must take into account:[2]

- Services performed

- Responsibilities involved

- Time spent

- Size and complexity of business

- Prevailing economic conditions

- Compensation paid by comparable firms for comparable services

- Salary paid to company officers in prior years

Example of savings: As a sole proprietor, your Schedule C income is $90,000 — all subject to social security taxes at 15.3% for a tax (after deduction of social security taxes) of $13,770. As an S Corporation employee, you earn $45,000 in wages and the balance as net income from use of capital assets. Your federal income tax is unchanged; however, your payroll tax is computed on $45,000 for a bite of:

Employer FICA	$3,442.50
Employee FICA	3,442.50
Total	$6,885.00

You save $6,890 ($13,770 - $6,885) by operating as an S Corporation rather than as a sole proprietor.

Strategy To Avoid Double Taxation

Strategy 4: Choose S Corporation status to avoid double taxation. Earnings of a regular corporation are taxed at the corporate level and then distributed to you as dividends. To avoid earnings at the corporate level, you must plan for zero earnings which is far easier said than done, especially if you are to avoid unreasonable compensation problems. Because S Corporation earnings flow through to you,[3] there's no double taxation problem with this form of business.

Strategy 5: Choose S Corporation status to shift income. One of the benefits of using an S Corporation is that all the income/loss flows through to the stockholders in proportion to their ownership. Thus, you may be able to shift income by giving some stock to your beneficiaries. Generally they get taxed on their share of undistributed income.[4] This is a *great* benefit, but you must be paid a reason- able wage[5] and you must treat other stockholders (i.g. your kids) as true stockholders. Thus, the income should be distributed (in pro- portion to their ownership) to their bank accounts. Do not use the money individually or put it back in the company.

Warning: The gift of S Corporation stock to shift future dividends is limited by the Kiddie Tax (see discussion on page 71). Thus, the benefit of income shifting using an S Corporation doesn't work well for kids under 14 years of age.

Strategy To Get Maximum Fringe Benefits

Strategy 6: Select regular corporation status for maximum fringe benefits.

Like a spouse: The sole proprietor must hire his or her spouse to obtain maximum fringe benefits such as fully deductible medical plans, etc. Think of the regular corporation as a spouse. With it, you can be the only employee and still qualify the corporation for, among others, fully deductible:

- Medical insurance plans[6]
- Medical reimbursement plans[7]
- Group insurance plans[8]
- Supper money[9]
- Meals and lodging for employer's convenience[10]

S Corporation gets fewer benefits: For fringe benefits, the S Corporation is treated by tax law the same as a partnership.[11] A person who owns more than 2% of the stock is treated like a partner in a partnership.[12] Partners are not entitled to tax-free employee fringe benefits and the partnership may not deduct the cost of such fringe benefits,[13] with the exception of medical insurance.

General Rules Of Thumb

1. High medical expenses — regular corporation

2. High disability premiums — regular corporation

3. Income $20,000 to $110,000 — S Corporation to save social security taxes

4. Use an S Corporation to shift income among family members

5. High liability exposure — corporation

6. Hiring children — sole proprietorship

7. Gift/Leaseback — any form, but assets must be owned individually to create benefits

8. Appreciating assets — S Corporation or proprietorship

Notes

Appendix A – Choosing The Right Business Form

1. IRS Publication 589 (Rev. Nov. 1992), Tax Information on S Corporations, p. 8.

2. Roob v. Commissioner, 50 T.C. 891, 898 (1968). See Radtke vs. U.S.; 712F. Supp. 143; Aff'd 895 F.2d 1196 (1990) in which no compensation was paid.

3. IRC § 1366(a).

4. § 1366 of IRC.

5. § 1366 (e) IRC.

6. IRC § 105.

7. Ibid.

8. IRC § 79.

9. IRC § 119.

10. Ibid.

11. S. Rep. No 640, 97th Congress, 2nd Session 1-26 (1982), Pg 3

12. IRC § 1372(b).

13. E.g., IRC § 703 "No deduction for medical expenses", IRC § 264(a)(1) "Life insurance not deductible if taxpayer financially interested."

Notes

B Appendix B - Estimated Taxes

Part I: Self-Employed Taxpayers

Overview: Most self-employed taxpayers and home based business owners must pay estimated taxes to the IRS or face a penalty. You are required to pay estimated tax if you expect to owe at least $1,000.[1]

Quarterly payments: You are normally required to compute your estimated taxable income and determine your expected tax liability on your expected income.[2] You would then make quarterly payments[3] by April 15, June 15, September 15, and January 15.

How to file estimated taxes: You pay all installments with IRS form 1040-ES.

Penalties: Failure to pay estimated taxes results in a penalty equal to the applicable short term interest rate plus three (3) percentage points.[4] As of January 2014, the underpayment penalty would be slightly less than 3.25%. This amount varies on a monthly basis as the Federal Short Term Interest Rate varies. This penalty is non-deductible.

Observation: Paying a 3% penalty that is nondeductible is like paying deductible interest of 4% at the 33% tax bracket. Thus, you might be willing to pay the penalty if your rate of return on your investments exceeds 4%.

Avoiding the penalty: There are three ways for individual taxpayers to avoid the penalty on failing to file estimated taxes. These are: the Guesstimate approach, the Safe Harbor approach, and the Annualization approach.

Guesstimate approach: We should note that the estimated tax needed to avoid penalty should be guessed within 90% of the tax to be owed this year, with payment made ratably during the year. Or, the taxpayer can pay in 90% of their 2013 tax obligation as a safe harbor as long as their adjusted gross income is less than $500,000 per year for married filing jointly and $250,000 for married filing separately.[5]

Note: The Guesstimate approach applies to all taxes including social security (FICA) taxes.[5]

Notes

Safe Harbor approach: The alternative and, in most cases the better approach, is to pay 100% of the tax shown on your prior year's tax return (adjusted for any amendments made). This approach is only available if a tax return was filed for the prior 12-month year.[6]

Example: Leslie had a $6,000 tax liability last year. If this year she wins the $68,000,000 Power Ball Lottery, she only needs to pay the $6,000 in estimated tax. The difference will be owed by April 15 of next year.

High Income Taxpayers: If your adjusted gross income last year exceeds $150,000 and less than two-thirds was from farming or fishing, the Safe Harbor approach is somewhat different. You must pay 110% of last year's tax to be safe.[7]

Example: Greg earned $520,000 as his adjusted gross income last year. After some deductions, his taxes were $48,000. If Greg wants to comply with the Safe Harbor rule, he would have to pay $52,800 at the rate of $13,200 per quarter.

Annualization Method: If you do not receive income evenly throughout the year and your income is expected to be less than last year, this might be the method for you.

Example: Scott is a golf instructor in Florida. The bulk of his income is earned from October to April. Scott may make smaller estimated payments in the summer months than during the winter months.

In short, the Annualization Method allows you to make payments as you earn your income. This method is similar to the Guesstimate approach. You would take your earnings for the year minus your expenses incurred to date and gross this amount up as if you will continue to earn this net income for the rest of the year.[8] Thus, your first installment is to be multiplied by 4 (since there are four quarters), the second installment is to be multiplied by 2, the third installment is to be multiplied by 1.5, and the final installment is to be multiplied by 1.

Example: From January 1 through March 31, Bill's adjusted gross income is $12,000. Using the Annualization method, Bill based his first installment as if he will earn $48,000 for the year and pays 25% of the tax for the first installment.

Note: Self-employment tax (FICA) has its own multiple which, due to the complexity of the calculation, is not worth separately computing. Just add the FICA tax to your income tax calculation.

Observation: The Annualization method is the most complicated of the three methods. It should only be used with some help from your accountant. If used correctly, however, it can be ideal for self-employed individuals whose income varies radically from year to year or whose income is earned seasonally.

Hot Tip: For most home based businesses, your income will not be earned seasonally and your income will probably increase each year (especially if residuals are involved). Thus, using the prior year's tax as a safe harbor is probably going to be the best approach.

Withholding can reduce estimated taxes: Any withholding on your wages or that of your spouse (if filing jointly) is treated as a payment of estimated taxes.[9] The major beneficial aspect of with-held taxes is that they are treated as withheld equally throughout the year regardless of when it was withheld.[10]

Example: Tony should pay $10,000 in estimated taxes in order to avoid any penalty. If Tony has $2,000 withheld from his wife's pay, he need only pay $8,000 in estimated taxes. However, if Tony's wife increases her withholding from September to December to equal the extra $8,000 required to be paid on estimates, Tony is not liable for any penalties. Notice that this is true even though most of the withholding occurred from September through December.

Hot Tip: If you have underpaid one or more installments and you have income subject to withholding, you may be able to retroactively avoid any estimated tax underpayment penalty by raising the amount withheld from either your check or that of your spouse's check. You could base the amount withheld on any of the above methods but using the Safe Harbor approach is probably best.

Part II: Estimated Tax Rules for Corporations

Overview: If you think that by incorporating you will avoid estimated tax, think again! Corporations also have to pay estimated taxes on a quarterly basis.[11] If your tax year ends on December 31, your payments are due: April 15, June 15, September 15, and December 15. If you have a different year-end than December 31, the due dates for the quarterly installments are as follows: May 15, July 15, October 15, and February 15.[12]

No penalty, however, is due if the tax shown on the return is less than $500.[13]

How to pay estimated taxes: Corporations pay estimated taxes by delivering each payment with Form 8109 to a qualified depository for federal taxes in your area.[14]

Methods to pay estimated taxes: There are four methods allowed by corporations:[15]

1. The Guesstimate Method
2. The Safe Harbor Method
3. The Annualized Income Method
4. The Seasonal Income Method

The Guesstimate Method: Under this method, you would pay 100% of the amount shown on your corporate tax return, prorated quarterly.[16] This method requires some guessing each quarter.

The Safe Harbor Method: You may avoid guessing by paying 100% of the tax shown on the return for the prior taxable year.[17] However, if your prior year's return was for less than 12 months or showed no tax due, you *cannot* use this method.[18]

Example: Widget Corp. reported a net loss last year and they paid no tax. Since they paid no tax on the prior year's return, they may not use the Safe Harbor Method.

Large corporations that had taxable income of $1,000,000 or more for any of the three immediate preceding tax years must use the Safe Harbor Method.[19]

Annualization Method: Corporations that are not large may also use the Annualization Method. If you want to avoid a headache and giving everyone around a headache, only use this method if your corporation's income dramatically varies from year to year and only if your corporation is on track to earn substantially less than last year.

Seasonal Method: This method can only be used if the corporation's income is earned primarily in one season; that is, if more than 70% of your income is earned seasonally this method might be beneficial.

It is similar to the Annualization Method but more complicated. You would use IRS Form 1120-W to determine your seasonally adjusted installments. Your accountant should compute each installment for you because of its inherent complexity.

Conclusion: Whether you are incorporated or self-employed, estimated taxes need to be paid if you want to avoid a penalty. Understanding these rules should ease your burden, help you avoid all underpayment of estimated tax penalties, and minimize what has to be paid to the IRS. This will keep more money in your pocket where it belongs!

Notes

Appendix B – Estimated Taxes

1. Section 6654 of the IRC and IRS Pub. 505(12/93) pgs. 18, 24.

2. IRS Pub 505(12/93) pg. 21.

3. IRS Pub 505(12/93) pg. 22.

4. Section 6621(a) of the IRC.

5. Section 6654(d)(1)(B)(i) of the IRC and IRS Pub. 505(12/94) pg. 21.

6. Section 6654(d)(1)(B)(2) of the IRC.

7. Section 6654(d)(1)(C)(i) of the IRC and IRS Pub. 505(12/93) pg. 18. See also TRA of 1997 § 1091.

8. IRS Pub 505(12/93) pg. 26.

9. Section 6654(g)(1) of the IRC.

10. Section 6654(g)(1) of the IRC.

11. Section 6655(c)(1) and (c)(2) of the IRC.

12. Section 6655(i)(1) of the IRC.

13. Section 6655(f) of the IRC.

14. Instruction from IRS Form 1120-W(1994) pg. 4.

15. Sections 6655(d)(1)(B) and 6655(e)(1)(A) of the IRC.

16. Section 6655(d)(1)(B)(i) of the IRC.

17. Section 6655(d)(1)(B)(ii) of the IRC.

18. Rev. Rul. 92-54, 1992-27, IRB 21.

19. Sections 6655(d)(2)(A) and 6655(g)(2) of the IRC.

C Appendix C - Business vs. Hobby Losses

Overview: Being in business is the last great tax reduction opportunity. If your business produces a loss, you may generally deduct that loss against any form of income.[1] This includes interest, dividends, rents, retirement and even that of your spouse's income (if you file jointly).

Carryback and carryforward of losses: if your losses exceed your income for the year 2015, you may carryback the eligible losses back 2 years, at your option, and receive a refund from the federal government (and many states) for the taxes paid during that carryback period; or you may carry the losses forward up to 20 years.

Example: David incurs a $10,000 loss from his business. If he earns $40,000 in wages, his taxable income would be $30,000.

Part II: Hobby Loss Rules

Overview: No deduction for losses for an activity are allowed for activities deemed hobbies or not engaged in for profit. In addition, no carryover of losses from hobbies is allowed.[4]

Example: Carrie has a business in travel that she operates from her home. Little time is spent in operating the business and little revenue is generated. If the IRS classifies her activities as a hobby, all losses from that business that exceed her income are disallowed.

Observation: For most home based businesses, reclassifying your activities from being a business to that of a hobby is the IRS's favorite weapon. It is *vital* that you learn to run your business like a business and not like a hobby.

Presumption of a profit: Congress has given all taxpayers a way to help solidify your business as a business and not be treated like a hobby. If your activity shows a profit for any three or more years in a period of five consecutive tax years, you are presumed to be engaged in a business.[5] IRS has a much tougher burden to prove otherwise.

Election to postpone IRS determination: You may elect to postpone any determination that your activities are a business or hobby until there are five consecutive tax years in existence from the time that you first engaged in the activity.[6]

Observation: There are several problems with making this election. First, it calls attention to yourself. Secondly, it extends the statute of limitations for several years. In short, do *not* make this election.

Criteria of business vs hobby: There are numerous standards that the courts use in determining whether your activities constitute a business or hobby. Generally, it is based on the facts and circumstances of each case.[7] You must show that you entered the activity with the objective of making a profit.[8] This is true even if there was a small chance of making a huge profit.

The majority of all court decisions indicate that you are required to have an honest profit objective when you undertake this venture. Thus, if you have a sincere purpose of eventually reaping an overall profit, you will be deemed to have a business motive.[9]

Tip: It is your motive at the time that you first start your endeavor that determines whether you have a business intent to make a profit. You should document this intent by sending a letter to your sponsor/company as to why you have entered this business emphasizing your desire to make a long-term profit and career out of this activity.

The courts have looked at the following factors in deciding if your endeavor is a business or a hobby:

1. Business plan: Most court decisions have looked favorably on taxpayers who prepare business plans showing projected estimated income and expenses of their endeavor.[10] The key is to project an *overall* business profit. In addition, the projected numbers should have some reasonable basis in reality. You should, therefore, document how you estimated each of your figures. You should also have a budget and an income statement from year to year, especially if you had losses in prior years. Furthermore, several recent cases require that your business plan should be individualized to you and NOT be a form document[10A]. It should include an analysis of the potential market and the time required to recoup startup costs, or the time and potential to achieve profitability.

HOT TIP: I have seen many cases turn in favor of the taxpayer primarily on a business plan. THIS IS CRUCIAL!

Observation: If your business contains inventories, you should certainly have enough inventory on hand to meet your goals.

2. Your own statements: IRS will use your own statements against you. Thus don't ever say, "I'm in this only to save taxes or costs, or to get a discount." In addition, don't have your business plan showing only estimated losses.[11]

146

3. Manner in which you conduct your activity: This is probably the single most important factor that IRS uses in judging a business intent from one where there is no expectation of profit. You must conduct your activity in a business-like manner. Thus, you *need to keep a diary* and maintain complete and accurate books and records.[12]

Tip: Keep separate books and records and bank accounts for your business.[13] Have your accountant do an annual review of your financial statements[10A]. Not only should you generate yearly income statements, but it is best if you have your accountant do a yearly review and make suggestions of where you can cut expenses and/or increase income. However, you don't need to cut expenses to the bone, but you do need to show that you made a business decision about each item of expense, especially if you are showing a loss.

4. Run your activity like a similar profitable business: You should also try to show that your activity is being carried on in a similar manner to other profitable activities.[14] Here is where the principle of duplication is critical. If you conduct your activity like other successful people in the same business, you have a stronger argument that you have conducted your activity like a business with the expectation of making a profit. In addition, if you follow the path of successful people, your chances of becoming successful are also enhanced. You might actually make a lot of money! You, therefore, want to adopt similar marketing efforts to those who are successful.[15] Thus, you should:

- Advertise your business
- Have business cards with your business and address on it
- Maintain a business telephone listing
- Purchase and use promotional literature
- Use a variety of marketing strategies[16]

5. Your prior business experiences can help or hurt: Your prior business experience in this industry can make a big difference to the IRS. If you have no prior experience in this endeavor, it is more questionable as to whether you ever had a profit motive.[17]

Note: The courts have held that this lack of prior business experience can be overcome by extensive study, listening to training tapes, taking seminars, attending training meetings, etc. Recent decisions have been favorably decided when taxpayers undergo extensive training either before they start their business or early in the business.

Morale: You can never get enough training! In addition, document all training and lectures attended. You should also document all help from other successful persons in your business. The documentation should be in your diary.

Notes

6. Thoroughly investigate your venture before starting it: Few good business people start a business without a good prior investigation of the business and any related companies. It is, therefore, very vital that you conduct a thorough prior investigation of your respective business and company prior to entering the business.[18]

7. Get expert advice: You should consistently consult with experts and other successful people or distributors in your business in order to constantly improve profits.[19] It goes without saying that you should document their advice and ordinarily follow the advice.

Meet with an accountant once a year: You need to produce yearly financial statements and 1099's. Some cases have noted that if you have losses, you should meet with your accountant at least once per year in order to decide what can be done to improve profitability. [19A] Don't ignore this!

Key: If you have losses, the courts seem to require that you are using your documents (such as financial statements, expenses spreadsheets, etc) as an analytical tool to make changes in your business. In addition, any Accountant or expert that you consult about potential business expense changes should NOT be in your upline. They should be an independent person. The reasoning for this is that the courts feel your upline has a vested interest in keeping you working regardless of your profitability. Whether you agree with these decisions or not, this is what the courts seem to determine.

8. Devote some time in a regular manner to your activity: Although you certainly do not need to conduct your activity full time, the more time and effort, the better. Cases have shown that as little as one hour per day on the average was substantial enough to support a profit motive.[20]

Observation: Businesses are conducted in a regular manner, hobbies are not. One hour a day for four days a week is better than eight hours once every two weeks.[21]

9. Your history of losses/income and steps taken to improve profits: Without question, your expenses can certainly exceed your income in a business. Absent unforeseen circumstances,[22] you should do everything to turn those losses into profits.[23] However, you should watch out for expenses that are unreasonably excessive when compared to your endeavor's income. Thus, in one case, an Amway distributor's accounting fees alone exceeded his entire gross income. There were other items of expenses that also grossly exceeded the income. The court held that the distributor's activities constituted a hobby and limited all deductions to that income. In fact, based on some recent cases,[24] the longer you have yearly losses (i.e. 3 years or longer) the more imperative it is to follow all the other factors mentioned in this chapter such as consulting with experts, changing your marketing, providing a business plan and yearly budgets, ect.

Observation: Based on numerous discussions with various IRS personnel, it seems that this concept of using excessive unreasonable expenses as a test for a lack of business profit motive, has been applied to a variety of endeavors. For example, one who enters the travel business and tries to deduct all their family trips despite very little gross income would have a tough time establishing that these trips have a profit motive. This is especially true if each trip was more than the gross income earned from the endeavor.

Note: Recent IRS cases note that although you do not have to make a profit, you should have *some* gross income yearly. If there is no income provided at all, this is indicative of a hobby.

It is essential that you document:

- All training
- Consultations with experts and other successful people in your business
- All marketing activities
- The reasons for all trips noting the business intent and the necessity for this trip

Note: Again, the important point is that your activity must be conducted in a business-like manner.

10. Amount of income from other sources: Although it may not seem fair, the greater your income from other sources, the less likely your loss from your activity may be deemed a business loss.[25] Although this is certainly not a determinative factor, if you have substantial other income from other activities, you need to more closely dot your i's and cross your t's.

11. Watch out for certain inherently suspicious activities:[26] Certain activities are inherently more suspect by the IRS because of significant personal pleasure involved. These include:

- Antique collecting
- Stamp collecting
- Traveling
- Writing
- Ministerial duties

- Record recording
- Raising show horses
- Training and showing dogs
- Automobile racing
- Home Based Business[27]

Tip: If you find yourself in one of the above mentioned activities, you must pay careful attention to the other business vs. hobby factors mentioned since your endeavor is inherently suspect.

Business vs. Hobby Loss Checklist

1. Try to have a profit in at least 3 out of 5 consecutive years. This is not mandatory, but nice to have.
2. Document business intent by sending a letter to your manager or sponsor/company as to why you have entered the business emphasizing your desire to make a long-term profit.
3. Make a business plan showing projected income/expense.
4. If your business contains inventory, always have enough on hand to justify your goals and business plan.
5. Don't make any improper statements such as "I'm in this only to save taxes."
6. Keep a good diary and maintain accurate books and records.
7. Utilize advertising, telephone business listings and a variety of marketing strategies.
8. Before entering your business, conduct an investigation of the industry and of any companies that you are thinking of associating with. Document your steps in this investigation.
9. Keep getting trained and getting tips on operating your business. This shows that you are constantly trying to make a profit.
10. Document any consulting with successful people or experts in your business.
11. Work your business regularly at least one hour a day, four to five times a week. This should be documented in your diary.
12. Clearly document the reason for making business trips.
13. Be especially careful if you are in one of the inherently suspicious activities.

Appendix C – Business vs Hobby Losses

1. Section 172 of the IRC and Regulations thereunder.
2. Section 172(b)(1)(A)(i) of the IRC. See also Taxpayer Relief Act (TRA) 1997 § 1082.
3. Section 172(b)(1)(A)(ii) of the IRC. See also Taxpayer Relief Act (TRA) 1997 § 1082.
4. Section 183(a) of the IRC and IRS Pub. 535 at pg. 5.
5. Section 183(d) of the IRC.
6. Section 183 of the IRC and S. Rept. No. 92-437 (PL 92 178) pg. 600; and S. Rept. No. 92-553 (Conference) (PL 92-178) pg. 663.
7. 1.183-2(a) of the Income Tax Regulations.
8. 1.183-2; Floyd Fisher, TC Memo 1980-183 (1980).
9. Maurice Dreicer, 78 TC 642, Affd. 702 F.2d 1205 (CA Dist Col. 1983).
10. Section 1.183-2(a) of the Income Tax Regulations; Jonas Bryant vs. Comm., 928 F.2d 745 (6th Cir. 1991).
10A. Smith vs. Commissioner, T.C. Memo 2007-154 (June 2007).
11. Harry Van Scoyoc, TC memo 1988-520 (1988).
12. 1.183-2(b)(i) of the Income Tax Regulations..
13. Frank Suiter, TC Memo 1990-447 (1990); Charles Givens, TC Memo, 1989-529 (1989); Joseph Ransom, TC Memo 1990-381 (1990) (Amway Distributor); Frank Harris, TC Memo 1992-638 (Mary Kay).
14. Section 1.183-2(b)(i) of the Income Tax Regulations..
15. C. Fink Fisher, 50 TC 164 (1968), Acq.
16. Sheldon Barr, TC Memo 1989-69 (1989).
17. Section 1.183-2(b) of the Income Tax Regulations; Joseph Ransom, TC Memo 1990-381 (1990); Abdolvahab Pirnia, TC Memo 1989-627.
18. Wenzel Tirheimer, TC Memo 1992-137 (1992).
19. Section 1.183-1(b)(2) of the Income Tax Regulations.
19A. Russel Kinney et. US vs. Commissioner T.C. Memo 2008-287.
20. Sherman Sampson, TC Memo 1982-276 (1982).
21. Percy Winfield, TC Memo 1966-53 (1966).
22. Section 1.183-2(b)(6) of the Income Tax Regulations.
23. Sections 1.183-2(b)(6)&(7) of the Income Tax Regulations.
24. Randall and Kay Olleff vs. Commissioner, T.C. Summary Opinion 2004-103
25. Section 1.183-2(b)(8) of the Income Tax Regulations.
26. Section 1.183-2(b)(9) of the Income Tax Regulations.
27. IRS Publication 4035 warns taxpayers of the potential dangers of Home Based Business scams.

Notes

D Appendix D - Tax Advantages of Qualified Plans

Introduction: I am constantly asked, "What one strategy would you recommend that all self-employed people utilize first?" Without question, if you are making over $25,000 a year of net income from your business, you MUST set up some sort of qualified pension or profit sharing plan. In addition, coupling it with an IRA would also be important.

Overview as to types of plans: Whether or not you have employees, and if you do, whether you wish to be generous to them or to make Scrooge seem like a charitable giver, there is a plan available to you. In this chapter, we will present an overview of the following plans:

- Simple Savings Plan (Simple IRA)

- Simple 401(k)

- Simplified Employee Pension (SEP)

- Qualified Profit Sharing Plan

- Qualified Money Purchase Plan

- Defined Benefit Plan

- Regular Individual Retirement Account

- Roth Individual Retirement Account

- Tax Exempt Education Individual Retirement Account

Note: There are more options such as ESOPS, VEBAs (for very high earning individuals), normal 401(k)s and more. Since these other plans aren't generally used by small businesses and home based businesses, they will not be discussed.

Strategy 1: Set up a qualified plan: There are many tax advantages of qualified plans: Without question, the main tax advantage is that you, the employer, get to deduct all contributions to the plan in the year of contribution[1] even if you don't get to benefit from it until sometime in the future.[2] In addition, all income earned by the plan is tax exempt[3] and, you are only taxed on the proceeds of the plan on the earlier of when they are actually distributed to you or when you reach a mandatory age for distribution of 70 1/2 (where you will be hopefully in a lower tax bracket).[4] Finally, you can name a beneficiary to receive the proceeds after death without incurring any gift tax.[5] Thus, there are many advantages to setting up a qualified plan.

Strategy 2: Set up a Simple Savings Plan (Simple IRA)

Introduction: One of the best ways to reduce taxes is to set up a qualified pension or profit sharing plan or 401(k). This will allow you to put away for your retirement as much as $12,500 maximum employee contribution in 2015 plus 3% of wages up to a maximum of $12,500 for the employer contribution. The problems with most qualified plans are that you can't just cover yourself and not cover the other full-time employees. In addition, even if you cover them, there is a top-heavy requirement. This means that if too much of the benefits go to you and the other employees do not participate enough, IRS can disqualify the plan. In addition, there are strict limits on plan investments. If there is a loss, you may be liable for the loss. Finally, there are onerous filing and administrative requirements that make these plans costly.

Congress, in an attempt to remedy these deficiencies, passed a Simple IRA plan. This plan eliminates the top-heavy requirements, and lessens the discrimination requirements, and almost eliminates most filings and administration.

What is it? A simple savings plan is a written arrangement that provides you and your employees with a simplified way to make contributions to provide retirement income. Under this plan, employees may choose whether to make salary deduction contributions rather than receiving salary. In addition, you must make some matching contributions on behalf of each eligible employee.[11]

Notes

Amount Contributed: An employee or self-employed person may contribute a percentage of salary or net income up to $12,000 in Compensation includes wages and for self-employed people means net earnings from self-employment.[13] You, the employer, must make matching contributions generally up to 3% of compensation. This amount may be as low as 1% for two years out of five.[14]

Note: Self-employed people may make contributions on their net income and provide the matching contributions for themselves. Also, for those ages 50 and over, in 2015 you may put in an extra $1,000 for IRAs as a catch up contribution and $3,000 for Simple IRAs, and $6,000 for SEPs and qualified plans.

Advantages of Simple Plans:

- No top-heavy rules for any year[15]

- Expanded types of investments over qualified plans

- There is almost no administrative cost or filing[16]

Notice to Employees: All employees must receive a notice as to requirements for eligibility, benefits, procedures for withdrawal, etc.[17] Use form 5305-SIMPLE (call 800-829-1040 for a copy).

Caution: This is limited to companies with 100 employees or fewer who make at least $5,000 in salary. Moreover, you can't use a simple IRA if you also have another qualified plan in effect.

Notes

Strategy 3: Set up a Simplified Employee Pension (SEP): In an attempt to eliminate many of the disadvantages with all 401(k)s, Congress passed a law allowing a SEP.

Advantages and disadvantages: SEPs are established by filing out IRS form 5305-SEP. You can get this form by calling IRS at "1-800-TAX-FORM!" This form is kept by you and NOT filed with the IRS. Thus, the cost of setup is negligible. In addition, like the simple savings plan, there is no IRS form to file annually. Thus, your annual maintenance costs are very low and are expected to be less than $500 annually (if that much). In addition, the contribution goes into each employee's IRA. Thus, each person can designate what investment to make and when to buy and sell. It is their IRA. Thus you have no investment problems or liabilities for bad investments. Finally, like profit sharing and simple savings plans, you can vary the investments from year to year. The funding is fully discretionary by you, giving you great flexibility from year to year.[9A] However, SEPs cannot be set up if you have leased employees.

Contributions to SEPs:

You are allowed to contribute 20% of your net earnings (which is stupidly computed after any contribution to the SEP) or wages up to a whopping $53,000 in 2015. This amount is indexed each year for inflation.[10]

Note: If you are incorporated or get a salary from a partnership, you are allowed to contribute 15% of your wages.

The main disadvantage, and this is a big one, is that this plan is nondiscriminatory.[11] You must cover anyone over age 21 who makes over $400 and has worked for you at least three years with some limited exceptions, and you cannot make any loans. The meaning of this is that if you have any employees, you may have to contribute 15% of their wages. You can, however, have a three-year waiting period before any vesting or contributions are made.

Observation: This is an ideal plan for self-employed individuals and home based business owners who don't have employees. It is cheap to set up and administer and hassle free. It is certainly one of my recommended plans of choice. In fact, even if you have employees and want to cover them, this is considered one of the better plans. On the other hand, if you have employees but you want to cover your employees as little as possible, stick to the Simplified Savings Plan noted above.

Qualified Profit Sharing Plans:

If flexibility is your need, this could be the plan of choice. You may contribute the same as a SEP, 20% of your net income up to a maximum contribution of $53,000 in 2015.[10] However, unlike other types of pension plans, profit sharing allows tremendous flexibility from year to year. If you want to contribute less than the maximum amount, you may. You may even contribute nothing for the year.

Advantages and disadvantages: Complete flexibility of contributions from year to year makes this plan very appealing. In addition, you make loans from the plan[12] and you can require a three-year waiting period before vesting any employee contributions. On the other hand, it is totally nondiscriminatory. Thus, if you have employees, you have to cover them by the same percentage. In addition, the costs of setting up the plan are estimated to be between $1,000–2,000 and the annual costs of administration and management can be several thousand dollars annually.

Observation: If you have a business that has tremendous variance in income from year to year, such as real estate, then this may well be the plan for you. This is especially true if you have no employees! I still believe, however, that either the Simplified Savings Plan or the SEP is a better plan due to the much lower costs involved coupled with the great flexibility of funding from year to year.

Qualified Money Purchase Plan:

This plan allows the second most contribution to the plan over any mentioned here. It allows up to a whopping 25% of wages up to a maximum contribution of $53,000 in 2015. For self-employed people, the limit is 20% of net income up to a maximum contribution of $53,000 in 2015. The maximum is increased each year for inflation.

Advantages and disadvantages: The maximum contribution to the plan is very appealing - not to mention that you can make loans and require a three year waiting period for employees to participate. However, the high costs of setup (which could be as high as $2,000) plus the high annual management costs, (which could be as high as several thousand dollars a year) should give you reason to pause. In addition, this plan has the least flexibility among any of the qualified plans. Once set up, you must contribute the set percentage noted in the plan forever for you and your employees. If you have employees, this can be a disaster since the contribution must be made even if you have a loss for the year.

Observation: Despite the higher contribution limits, I would stay away from this plan if you have any employees or are thinking of ever having any employees in the future.
If however, you have a business whose income doesn't vary from year to year (lucky you!), and are feeling really generous to your staff, this plan could be the right one for you.

Defined Benefit Plan: The maximum contribution is a whopping $210,000 in 2015.

In most other plans, you contribute a set percentage of your net income or wages to the plan. This is not true in a Defined Benefit Plan. Here, you set up what amount of retirement income that you want and an actuary figures out how much to contribute.

Advantages and disadvantages: The older you are, the more you can contribute. It also allows for a higher annual income flow to your employees. However, it is by far the most expensive form of pension since it needs an actuary. These plans can run as much as $10,000 a year to manage and administer.

Observation: Unless you want lots of hassles, stay away from this plan. You can contribute more money beyond the normal pension contributions with an IRA or a VEBA (Voluntary Employee Benefits Association).

Strategy 4: Set up an Individual Retirement Account (IRA)

Overview: The use of an IRA has been greatly improved by the Taxpayer Relief Legislation for 1998 and thereafter. In fact, many people who have been active participants in qualified plans may now also participate in an IRA.

Active participation in a qualified plan by both you and your spouse: Generally, IRAs can be set up if either you or your spouse is not covered by a qualified plan (i.e. SEP, pension, 401(k) etc.).

However, even if both you and your spouse are active participants in a qualified plan, you may also set up an IRA if your adjusted gross income is less than the following:

Year	Single Taxpayers[13]	Married Filing Jointly[14]
2015	$61,000 - $71,000	$98,000 - $118,000

Only one spouse is covered by a qualified plan: If you are married and only one spouse is covered by a qualified plan, you may set up an IRA of up to $5,500 in 2015 for the spouse who is not an active participant in a qualified plan if your 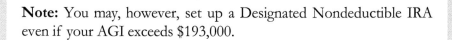 combined adjusted gross income (AGI) is under $183,000. However, if your combined AGI exceeds $183,000, your $5,500 IRA availability starts phasing out and completely phases out at $193,000 of AGI.

Note: You may, however, set up a Designated Nondeductible IRA even if your AGI exceeds $193,000.

Notes

Withdrawals from IRAs: Normally you may not withdraw any money from an IRA until you reach at least 59 1/2 without a penalty. However, there are several exceptions that allow premature withdrawal of your IRA funds prior to age 59 1/2 without any penalty.

First time homebuyer exception: First time homebuyers may withdraw up to $10,000 once during their lifetime[15] to pay for acquiring or constructing or reconstructing a principal residence.[16] In addition, the distribution from the IRA must be used by you or your family within 120 days upon which the payment is received. Your family includes you, your spouse, a child, a grandchild, an ancestor of you or your spouse.[17]

Example: Sam took $10,000 out of his IRA to help fund the down payment for his daughter's first home. Sam may never use this exception again.

Hot tip: Although it is not clear from the 1997 tax act or conference reports, it seems that both you and your spouse can use this exception. Thus, if you are married, you and your spouse may each take advantage of this exception out of your respective IRAs.

Higher Education Exception: A further exception applies to all IRAs for distributions to pay for qualified higher education expenses.[18] Qualified expenses include college, graduate school, room, books, fees, supplies, and equipment required for attendance or enrollment.[19] These expenses can also be used for you, your spouse, any child or grandchild of you or your spouse.[20]

Cautionary note: Although not subject to penalties, all withdrawals from IRAs due to the exceptions noted are subject to income taxation except withdrawals from Roth IRAs (to be discussed below).

TYPES OF IRA ACCOUNTS

Deductible IRAs: This is known as your traditional IRA. It allows you to fund and deduct up to $5,500 in 2015 for you and for your spouse subject to certain income limits noted above if you or your spouse is a active participant in a qualified plan.[21] However, all withdrawals for any reason are fully taxable. The investment build-up, like all qualified plans, remains untaxed until withdrawal.

Strategy 5: Set up a Roth IRA: Unlike the traditional IRA, contributions to the Roth IRA are nondeductible. Thus, why would anyone want to set up a Roth IRA and not get a deduction? The reason is that, if you meet certain conditions, <u>all withdrawals for either retirement or for an exception allowing premature withdrawals are tax free</u>.[21]

Contributions: You may contribute the lessor of any compensation received or $5,500 in 2015.[22] Moreover, any amount put into a deductible IRA reduces what you can contribute to the Roth IRA.

Unfortunately, in 2015 the Roth IRA phases out when you start earnings over:[23]

<u>Single</u>	<u>Married filing jointly</u>
$116,000–$131,000	$183,000–$193,000

These phaseout limits apply whether or not you are an active participant in a qualified plan. Congress obviously ignored any attempt at keeping this simple.

Observation: Roth IRAs are better in my opinion than any other form of IRA, even one that is deductible. When possible, this is the one IRA that should be funded by you if you are eligible.

Rollovers to Roth IRAs: Interestingly, you may rollover your traditional IRA into a Roth IRA without penalty.[24] There is also no income limitations for the Roth rollover. Thus, anyone can make this qualified rollover contribution without penalty.[25]

There is a drawback to rolling over your traditional IRA into a Roth IRA. Your rollover is subject to normal income tax (Yuck).[27]

Distributions from Roth IRAs: Distributions from Roth IRAs are not taxable[28] if the Roth IRA has been in existence for five(5) years and either:

- you become age 59 1/2, or

- you die (not my favorite exception), or

- you become disabled, or

- you use the money for one of the premature withdrawal exceptions.

Strategy 6: Set up a Coverdale IRA

Overview:

This is an IRA that must be used exclusively for qualified higher education expenses for you or your family.[29] Qualified higher education expenses include tuition, room, board, fees, supplies, and equipment needed for enrollment or attendance.[30]

Contribution: Contributions are generally nondeductible and in addition to any other IRA of up to $2,000 per student.[31] Moreover, the contributions must be made before the due date for your income tax return (normally April 15).[32]

Sadly, what Congress gives they also take away. In 2015, the annual $2,000 contribution limit per beneficiary is phased out ratably for contributors with modified AGI of:[33]

Single Taxpayers	Married Filing Jointly
$110,000	$220,000

Treatment of Distributions:

If your beneficiary's qualified education expenses equals or exceeds the education IRA's distribution for the year, the distribution is tax free.[34] However, if the distribution exceeds the amount of the qualified education expenses, a portion of the excess distribution will be taxable.[35]

Observation: You have nothing to lose by setting up this type of IRA for educational expenses if you qualify. It does not reduce what you can contribute to another type of IRA. Thus, the moral of this story is that if you qualify for an education IRA and have family members who will use the money for qualified higher education expenses, this is one IRA that should almost always be set up.

Notes

Strategy 7: Hire your kids and let them set up the IRA: If you are making sufficient income as to not qualify for an education IRA, there is a great way around these prohibitions. Hire your children!! They can use the wages to fund their own Roth IRA and education IRA. You would effectively get the same benefits!!

Strategy 8: When all else fails, set up a Designated Nondeductible IRA: If you can't qualify for any of the other IRAs mentioned above and you don't want to hire your kids or don't have kids, your IRA of last resort is a Designated Nondeductible IRA (DNIRA). The good news is that it is available to anyone regardless of income if you didn't fund another type of IRA (other than an education IRA which is in addition).[36] The bad news is that the contributions are nondeductible and when distributions are made, the income earned by the IRA is taxable ratably.

Contributions: The allowable contributions are the same as most of the other IRAs: the lessor of your compensation or $4,000.[37] You actually elect to have your contributions as nondeductible by filing IRS form 8606 with your tax return.

Observation: If you aren't eligible to set up a Roth IRA or a traditional IRA, this type of IRA should be set up. However, it is clearly the choice of last resort.

Strategy 9: Don't forget the Saver's Tax Credit which could be as much as 50% of the first $2,000 of pension or IRA contributions for you and your spouse ($1,000 for single taxpayers).[20] However, the catch is that you must earn less than the following AGI in 2015[39].

2015						
Joint Return		Head of Household		Married Filing Separate		Applicable Percentage
Over	Not Over	Over	Not Over	Over	Not Over	
0	$36,500	0	$27,375	0	$18,250	50%
$36,500	$39,500	$27,375	$29,625	$18,250	$19,750	20%
$39,500	$61,000	$29,625	$45,750	$19,750	$30,500	10%
$61,000	-	$45,750	-	$30,500	-	0%

Strategy 10: If you are 50 or over, you may make an extra catch up contribution to most retirement plans.

Traditional IRA & Roth IRA	
2014	$1,000
2015	$1,000
Simple IRA	
2014	$2,500
2015	$3,000
401(k), SEP's, Qualified Plans	
2014	$5,500
2015	$6,000

SUMMARY

- **Strategy 1**: You absolutely need a qualified plan if you are making over $25,000 of net income since the contributions are tax deductible.

- **Strategy 2:** Set up a Simple Savings Plan. Simple Savings Plans allow up to $12,500 maximum employee contribution in 2015 plus 3% of wages up to $12,500 more for the employer contribution, and are simple and are very cheap to maintain. There are very little contributions that need be made to employees. Highly recommended if you have employees.

- **Strategy 3**: Set up a SEP. SEPs are among the best and usually the plan of choice. SEPs are cheap, allow up to $53,000 in 2015 per year into the plan and are flexible. However, you must put up to 25% of other employees' wages into plan. This is considered the best qualified plan if you have no employees or few employees.

- Simple 401 (k) are good but not cheap to maintain. Generally, SEPs are better.

- Qualified Profit Sharing plans allow for flexibility of contributions from year to year but are expensive to maintain and nondiscriminatory. For most small and home based business, this should not be used.

- Qualified Money Purchase Pension plans allow for larger contributions (up to $53,000 in 2015) but are expensive to maintain and nondiscriminatory. I recommend that unless you have no employees or want to be overly generous, don't utilize this plan.

- **Strategy 4**: Set up an IRA (Individual Retirement Account).

- **Strategy 5**: Set up a Roth IRA. This results in tax free distributions for retirement, education, and first time home-buyers.

- **Strategy 6**: Set up an education IRA.

- **Strategy 7**: Hire your kids and let them set up the IRA.

- **Strategy 8**: When all else fails, set up a Designated Nondeductible IRA.

- **Strategy 9**: Don't forget to take the retirement savings credit.

- **Strategy 10**: Don't forget to make an extra catch-up contribution if you are 50 or over.

Appendix D – Tax Advantages for Qualified Plans

1. § 404(a) of the Internal Revenue Code.

2. § 404(a) of the IRC.

3. Ibid; § 403, 401(a) of the IRC.

4. § 402(a); 402(b); 403 of the IRC.

5. § 402(d); 403 of the IRC.

6. § 408(p)(6)(B) of the IRC. Rev Proc 2012-52

7. § 401(k)(II)(B(ii)(II) of the IRC.

8. § 401(k)(D)(ii) of the IRC.

9. Rev. Proc. 2012-52.

9a. § 408(k)(6)(D) of the IRC.

10. IRS Pub. No. 560, Page 4.

11. IRS Pub. No. 560, Page 4. See also § 408(k)(2)(A), 408(k)(2)(B) of the IRC.

12. § 408(e) and 72(p)(2)(A) of the IRC; IRC 2000-82 (11/20/2000). See also IRC 2003-122 (10/16/2003)

13. § 219(g)(3)(b) of the IRC.

14. IBID.

15. Section 72(t)(8)(B) of the IRC.

16. § 72(t)(2)(F) & § 72(t)(8)(B) of the IRC.

17. Section 72(t)(8)(A) of the IRC; IR 2012-77.

18. Section 72(t)(2)(E) of the IRC.

19. Section 293, H.R. 2014 Committee Reports of Taxpayer Relief Act of 1997.

20. Section 72(t)(7)(H) of the IRC.

21. Section 219 of the IRC.

22. Section 408(A)(c)(I) of the IRC.

23. § 408(c)(C)(ii) of the IRC.

24. § 408(A)(d)(3)(A)(ii) of the IRC.

25. § 408(c)(3)(B)(i) of the IRC. Modified by IRS notice 2009-75, Sect III Q&A 2(a), 2009-39 IRB 436.

26. § 408(A)(c)(B)(ii) of the IRC.

27. Intentionally left blank.

28. § 408(A)(d)(I)(A) of the IRC.

29. § 530(b)(I) of the IRC.

30. § 530(b)(2), 529(e)(3) of the IRC.

31. § 530(b)(I)(A) of the IRC.

32. § 530(d)(4)(C) of the IRC.

33. § 532(c)(2) of the IRC.

34. § 530(d)(2)(A) of the IRC.

35. § 530(d)(2)(B) of the IRC.

36. § 408(o)(2)(c)(i) of the IRC.

37. § 408(o)(2)(B)(i) of the IRC.

38. IRS Section 25(B) of the IRC.

39. Rev. Proc.2012-52.

E Appendix E - When a Charitable Contribution Can Be a Deductible Business Expense

Introduction: A rose may be a rose by any name, but a charitable gift may not always be a charitable contribution. Most charitable gifts are not business deductions. However, there are occasions where a gift can constitute a business deduction.

Advantages of being a business deduction: If a charitable gift can be treated as a business deduction, there are several advantages:

- The gift reduces the net income for FICA savings 15.3% on the first $118,500 of net earnings in 2015.

- The gift reduces the Medicare premiums for any net earnings above $118,500.

- Business expenses are generally deductible in full while charitable deductions have limits.

IRS position of charitable gifts being business expenses: IRS has mandated that most charitable gifts are not business expenses. However, a gift can be a business expense when:

1. There is a direct relationship between your business and the gift, and

2. You have a reasonable expectation of a direct financial return that is commensurate with the amount of the donation.[1]

The mark of Marquis: The leading case in this area is based on Sarah Marquis.[2] Marquis was involved in a travel agency that conducted 57% of its business with a charitable organization. In addition, new contributions to the charity were directly related to the amount and profitability of the business given the agency by the charity. The tax court held that despite no binding obligation to make a gift, all gifts by the travel agency to the charitable organization were substantial and an integral part of its business and there- fore deductible as a business expense.

Hot tip: If you want a charitable gift to be deemed a business expense, you must *clearly* demonstrate that your payments to the charity are directly related to the business produced by the charity for you and such payments are made to either induce continuing business by the charity or result in some direct, immediate financial benefit to your business. In addition, there should be a proven direct relationship between the amount given and the business conducted.[3]

Example: Sam provides phone service to a charity. The charity is constantly giving Sam more customers. Sam should pay to the charity a fixed percentage of all customer billing to the charity in order to safely establish a reasonable expectation of a direct financial return commensurate with the business generated.

Warning: It is important to establish that the benefit to the business is immediate and does not provide a benefit whose return is too remote.[4]

Documentation: Sam should write a letter to the charity noting that he will give a fixed percentage of the business generated to the charity as a thank you. In addition, it is important to treat the gift as a business expense on the books. The bean counters must record it correctly or IRS will hold this against you.

Notes

Appendix E – When a Charitable Contribution Can Be a Deductible Business Expense

1. Sections 1.162-15(b) and 1.170A-1(c)(5) of the Regulations.

2. <u>Sarah Marquis</u>, 49 TC 695 (1968); <u>Acq.</u> 1971-2 CB 3.

3. <u>Adeline Marcell</u>. <u>Admrx vs. U.S.</u> 8 AFTR 2d. Par. 5344 (DC VT. 1961).

4. <u>Pensacola Greyhound Racing, Inc.</u>, TC Memo 1973-225 (1973).

Notes

F Appendix F — Educational Overview

There are three new changes to the tax law that allow either a deduction or tax credits. As a reminder, a tax credit is better than a deduction in that it is a dollar for dollar reduction in taxes. Thus, a $1,000 tax credit reduces your federal taxes by $1,000.

1. American Opportunity Credit[1] (Known as the "Hope Credit"): In 2015, taxpayers can get 100% of first years qualified education expenses up to $2,000 and 25% of any expenses thereafter up to a maximum yearly credit of $2,500 per student! Qualified expenses include tuition, required fees, and now mandatory materials used in the course.

Second, the credit is available for each year of college up to the first four years. It was only available for the first two years of college previously.

Third, what Congress gives, they take back. The credit is phased out for married taxpayers filing joint returns at $160,000 - $180,000 of MAGI, and phases out for single filers from $80,000 to $90,000

Note: The American Opportunity Credit doesn't apply to a student who has been convicted of a federal or state felony dealing with drugs. Presumably, if your kids are hired hit-men, this would be fine. This is an example of the extreme stupidity of Congress!

2. Lifetime Learning Credit[1]: You may also get a lifetime learning credit for $2,000 per year for both undergraduate and graduate education. Again, what Congress gives, they take back. The credit is phased out for married taxpayers filing joint returns at $110,000 of income or $55,000 of income for single taxpayers in 2015. Fortunately, unlike the Hope credit, this credit can be used every year, not just for the first four years.

Note: Neither the American Opportunity credit nor the lifetime learning credit can be used for educational expenses paid by an educational IRA.

Caution: The American Opportunity credit are available on a per student basis. Thus, if you have three children in college, you can get three American Opportunity credits. However, the yearly lifetime learning credit is per *taxpayer*. Thus, under the same circumstances, you will get one lifetime learning credit per year.

Note: Unlike the American Opportunity Credit, the Lifetime Learning Credit is available to convicted drug felons.

Tip: You may claim *both* the American Opportunity credit and the lifetime learning credit for more than one eligible student in the same year.[2]

3. Student Loan Interest: You can deduct interest on qualified education loans. It is $2,500 for years 2001 and later. Sadly, this deduction is phased out for single taxpayers whose modified adjusted gross income in 2015 is over $65,000 and totally phases out at $80,000. The phase- out limit for married taxpayers filing jointly is $130,000 - $160,000[3]. The interest is deductible over any time period.

Appendix F - Educational Overview

1. H.R. Report #220, 105th Congress, 1st Session (1997).
   See also, Notice 97-60, § 2; Q&A 6, 1997-46, IRB 8.
   Rev Proc 2012-52,

2. IRS Publication Number 970 (2/98) page 4; and Conf. Report
   Number 105-220 (PL 105-34) Page 346.

3. § 221(a) and 221(b)(1) of the IRC. See also Rev. Proc. 2012-52..

Appendix G — Disabled or Blind Dependents

A new kind of saving program (ABLE Account) was established to provide support for individuals with disabilities who are unable to work.

Maximum Contribution: Up to $14,000 per year for each qualified disabled person. The contribution to these accounts must be in cash and NOT in property. They can start in 2015 and thereafter.

Tax free earnings if used for qualified expenses: The earnings on this account are tax free if used for qualified expenses. However, if the account balance exceeds $100,000, they may not be eligible to receive supplement security income that can be paid to disabled or blind taxpayers. They can, however, be eligible for Medicaid and the account will not be used to prevent Medicaid qualification.

What are qualified expenses: These accounts can be used to pay for the following:
- Education
- Housing
- Transportation
- Employment training and support
- Assistive technology and personal support services
- Health, prevention, and wellness
- Financial management fees and administrative services
- Legal fees
- Funeral and burial expenses
- Other expenses approved by IRS

Who is eligible for this: This is an individual who during the tax year is either blind or so disabled as to be eligible to receive Social Security Disability income.

Sandy's Tip: This means that they can't hold or job or work at any gainful employment due to their disability. Also, a disability certification must be filed with the IRS by either the individual or their parent or guardian confirming they meet the qualification. The certification must include a copy of the individual's diagnosis relating to any relevant impairment and signed by a licensed physician.

Finally, the individual's disability must have occurred before they reach age 26.

Sandy's elaboration: These accounts are most useful for conditions that have early onset, such as Down Syndrome, Autism, Cerebral Palsy, birth defects, etc. Sadly, they won't be useful for conditions that arise later in life.

How are these account set up: Like prepaid tuition accounts, these accounts will be set up by the states. However, if you or the beneficiary moves states, a 60-day rollover to the new account can be made on a tax free basis.

What happens on death of the beneficiary: Any funds supplied by Medicaid will be reimbursed to the government up to the amount in the account. Any excess amounts will be included in the estate of the deceased. The accumulate earnings will be subject to income tax.

ABLE accounts are exempt from bankruptcy: If a parent or grandparent contribute funds to the ABLE account and then subsequently declare bankruptcy, these funds will be protected from bankruptcy as long as the contribution was made at least 365 days before filing bankruptcy.

Notes

Glossary

A 401(k) plan: This is a defined contribution plan allowed under section 401(K) of the Internal Revenue Code.

Amortization: The reduction of the value of an asset by prorating its cost over a period of years.

An HSA: This stands for a "Health Savings Account," which is a trust set up to pay qualifying medical and dental expenses.

Bonus Depreciation: This is a special amount of the purchase price of a newly purchased business asset that can be immediately expensed. It only applies to new equipment and is in addition to the expense allowance that can be used for used equipment purchases.

Business Club: Organizations that further the business interest of their members. Examples would be "exchange clubs," "Rotary," and Chamber of Commerce.

Convention: A formal meeting of members, representatives, or delegates, as of a political party, fraternal society, profession, or industry.

Depreciation: A reduction in the value of an asset with the passage of time, due in particular to wear and tear.

Documentation system: A compilation of records, files and other backup material needed to support a deduction or tax credit.

Entertainment: Something affording pleasure, diversion, or amusement, especially a performance of some kind that is designed to enhance business or build a business relationship.

Expense Allowance: This is an election made by small businesses to deduct the purchase of new equipment instead of taking depreciation and is allowed under section 179 of the Internal Revenue Code.

Flexible Spending Plan: This is also known as a Cafeteria plan. This is an employee benefit plan that allows staff to choose from a variety of benefits to formulate a plan that best suits their needs. Cafeteria plan options may include health and accident insurance, cash benefits, tax advantages and/or retirement plan contributions

Gift: Something voluntarily transferred by one person to another without compensation and given with disinterested generosity.

Home Office: A place in your principal residence where you perform your most important functions for a business or where you perform substantially all of your administrative tasks for a business.

IRS standard mileage Rates: This is a per business mile deduction that is allowed instead of deducting certain actual vehicle expenses of gas, oil, repairs, depreciation, insurance, cleaning and waxing costs.

IRS Standard travel Rates: In lieu of keeping expenses for meals, lodging and travel, IRS provides high and low cost standard rates for meals, lodging, and incidental expenses for any business trip.

Luxury Boat: Any cruise ship. This term would also include ships rented for business or personal trips.

On-the-road expenses: Costs necessary to sustain life while on a business trip. These include lodging, meals, laundry, dry cleaning, shoe shines and similar expenses.

Real estate caretaking travel: Any trip designed to participate in the management, sale or repair of rental or commercial property.

Roth 401(k): A 401(K) plan that does not provide a deduction for contributions but can result in tax free distributions upon retirement.

Roth IRA: A Individual Retirement account that does not provide a deduction for contributions but can result in tax free distributions upon retirement.

Self-Insured Medical Plan: A written plan that provides reimbursement for qualified medical and dental expenses that are not covered by insurance.

Seminar: Any group or meeting for holding discussions, getting educated or exchanging information.

Sole proprietorship: A self-employed taxpayer or independent contractor that files an IRS Schedule C.

Tax Diary: An organized tracking system containing business expenses and the necessary questions required by the Internal Revenue Service.

Transportation Expenses: Expenses incurred in getting to and from your destination.

Index

Visit our web site at: www.taxreductioninstitute.com

Visit our web site at: www.taxreductioninstitute.com